mastering herringbone stitch
THE complete GUIDE

INTERWEAVE.
interweave.com

MELINDA BARTA
Editor of *Beadwork* magazine

editor
MICHELLE MACH

technical editor
MINDY BROOKS

associate art director
JULIA BOYLES

photographer
JOE COCA

additional photography
ANN SABIN SWANSON

photo stylist
EMILY SMOOT

design
PAMELA NORMAN

layout
COURTNEY KYLE

illustrator
BONNIE BROOKS

production
KATHERINE JACKSON

Interweave
A division of F+W Media, Inc.
201 East Fourth Street
Loveland, CO 80537
interweave.com

Manufactured in China
by RR Donnelley Shenzhen

Library of Congress Cataloging-in-
Publication Data
Mastering herringbone stitch : the
complete guide / [compiled by]
Melinda Barta.
pages cm
Includes bibliographical references
and index.

ISBN 978–1–59668–632–8 (pbk.)
ISBN 978-1-62033-471-3 (PDF)

1. Beadwork—Patterns.
2. Weaving. 3. Stitches (Sewing) I.
Barta, Melinda A., editor of compilation.

TT860.M35 2014
746.5—dc23

2013023642

10 9 8 7 6 5 4 3 2 1

Dedication
For my mom, Jean

Thanks

Foremost, thank you to the gifted designers who created many of the lovely and enticing projects you'll find in this book. This includes *Beadwork* Designers of the Year Jean Campbell, Leslie Frazier, Lisa Kan, Carole Ohl, Jean Power, Kelly Wiese, and Jill Wiseman.

I sincerely thank all of the wonderful designers, beaders, vendors, illustrators, photographers, and editors who contributed their talent, unmatched creativity, and eagle eyes to this book. This includes Marlene Blessing, Bonnie Brooks, Mindy Brooks, Joe Coca, Allison Korleski, Kerry Jackson, Michelle Mach, Pamela Norman, Katie Nelson, Vicki Star, Ann Swanson, Rachel Ure, and the entire Interweave staff.

And last but certainly not least, I thank my entire family for their love and encouragement.

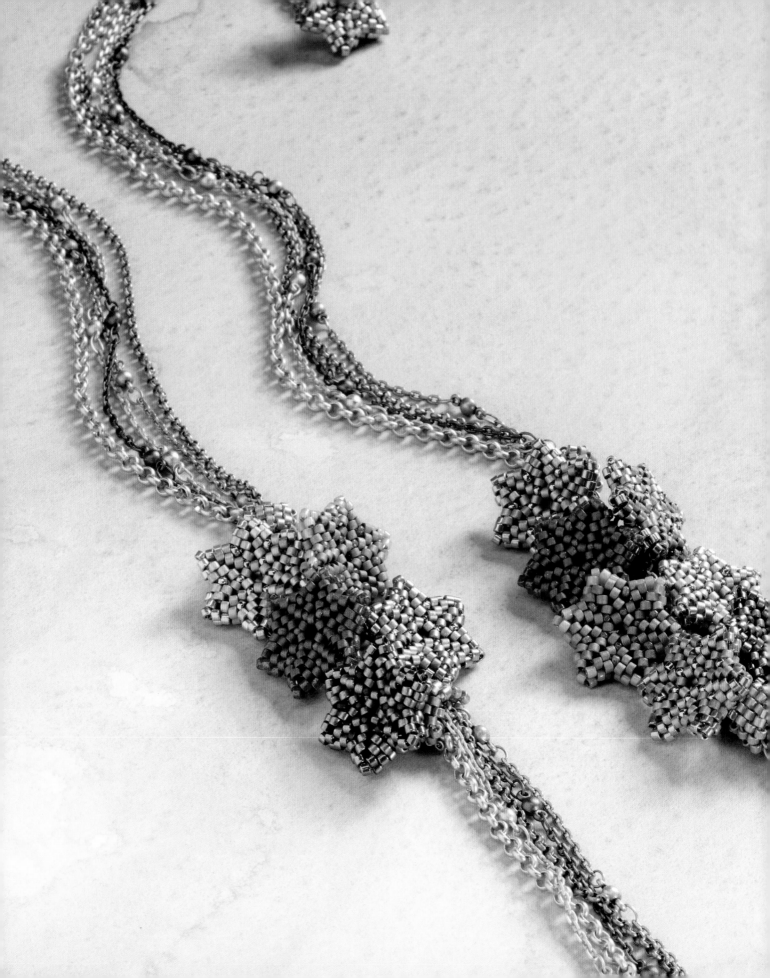

As editor of *Beadwork* magazine, I encounter everything from cubic right-angle weave to Russian spiral to soutache embroidery on any given day. Although I appreciate the unique construction of every stitch, herringbone is one of my true loves because its versatility and distinctiveness never cease to amaze me. To me, herringbone has its own personality. It can be quiet and subtle—such as when worked in a rope with size 15°s—or bold and loud with its noticeably angled beads—such as when worked in a flat band where its unmistakable pattern shines.

Even the origin of its name is unusual. Herringbone stitch is also known as Ndebele, named after the South African tribe credited with developing the stitch. It's most often worked in rows with two beads in each stitch. Work several rows and watch the beads begin to stack in columns, with beads that angle away from each other, resembling the bones of a fish skeleton (such as herring, hence the name's origin). Place several of these columns side by side and notice the resemblance to herringbone fabric and some decorative tile work. The pattern itself is rich in history; artifacts with this pattern date back to ancient Egypt and perhaps even earlier.

This book will expose you to absolutely everything you need to know about beading this timeless stitch. From basic materials and your first stitch to advanced shaping techniques, this comprehensive guide contains more than just a collection of great designs. Start by turning to the Basics for an overview of beading, findings, and tools. Here, you will also find Must-Know Terms (which guide you through the terminology used in the instructions) and Beading 101 (including an elementary start to herringbone). As the book progresses from flat to circular to tubular herringbone stitches, check each section opener for more detailed how-tos on each stitch variation. Plus, don't miss the sections dedicated to fun spirals and twists and adding finishing touches to your work. Information on other stitches commonly combined with herringbone—including square stitch, peyote stitch, right-angle weave, and more—can be found in the Beyond the Basics section near the end of the book. Here, you'll also find instructions for crimping, wireworking, and knotting.

Not only am I thrilled to bring you every variation and technical aspect of herringbone I could possibly think of all in one book, but I'm also excited to include designs from seven all-star contributors. In addition to my own designs, guest contributors Jean Campbell, Leslie Frazier, Lisa Kan, Carole Ohl, Jean Power, Kelly Wiese, and Jill Wiseman—all known for their time spent as *Beadwork* Designers of the Year—share projects that reflect their matchless beading styles, deep knowledge of beadweaving, and excellence in teaching.

Whether you bead only one project or all of them, I invite you to enjoy all of the wonderfully diverse variations that result from just this one stitch.

Have fun!
Melinda

basics

This handy guide to beadweaving and jewelry making welcomes you to the wonderful world of herringbone stitch. Start off with an overview of bead types and the most common findings and tools. Do you sometimes feel as if we beaders speak our own language? Then don't miss the list of must-know terms on page 18. Beading 101 (page 19) covers everything from threading your needle to maintaining perfect thread tension. For herringbone stitch basics, turn to page 22. Don't miss the Beyond the Basics section that begins on page 158, where you'll learn to combine herringbone with other stitches, including peyote stitch, right-angle weave, square stitch, and more. And last but not least is a lesson on crimping, wireworking, and knotting (page 161) because, even if you bead strictly with seed beads, many of these techniques are necessary for designing and finishing your work.

Let's get started!

BEADS

seed beads

Seed beads are made of glass and come in a variety of shapes, sizes, colors, and finishes. They are sized on an inverse scale: the larger the number, the smaller the bead. Seed beads range from size 2° (largest) to 24° (smallest).

Aught describes a seed bead's size and is usually represented by a small degree symbol. The exact origin of this symbol is unknown, but it is thought to have once referred to how many strands of beads occupy 1" (2.5 cm) when lined up side by side. For example, eleven parallel strands of size 11°s (or eleven size 11°s laid side by side, not hole to hole) would equal 1" (2.5 cm).

Czech seed beads

Most **Czech** seed beads are sold prestrung in twelve-strand bundles called hanks. A typical hank of size 11° seed beads measures about 10" (25.5 cm) long (20" or 51 cm of beads per looped strand); hanks of size 13° charlottes, a faceted bead, are about 6" (15 cm) long (12" or 30.5 cm per looped strand). One hank of size 11°s weighs about 35 to 45 grams. Manufactured in the Czech Republic, the beads on these hanks are temporarily strung on thin thread and must be restrung or transferred onto a stronger thread or wire. Czech seed beads are very round and donutlike and, when compared to cylinder beads and Japanese seed beads, are quite inconsistent in size. This isn't a bad thing—sometimes a bead that's a little too wide or a little too skinny will be just what you need.

SIZE CHART

		1"
7	◎ ☐☐☐☐☐☐☐☐☐	
8	◎ ☐☐☐☐☐☐☐☐☐☐	⊢————1"————⊣
9	◎ ☐☐☐☐☐☐☐☐☐☐☐	11° Japanese seed beads About 17 per inch
10	◎ ☐☐☐☐☐☐☐☐☐☐☐☐	
11	◎ ☐☐☐☐☐☐☐☐☐☐☐☐☐	⊢————1"————⊣
12	◎ ☐☐☐☐☐☐☐☐☐☐☐☐☐☐☐	12° Czech seed beads About 21 per inch
14	◎ ☐☐☐☐☐☐☐☐☐☐☐☐☐☐☐☐☐	

cylinders

Japanese seed beads

bugles

Cylinder beads are perfectly cylindrical Japanese beads. Brands include Delica (made by Miyuki), Aiko and Treasure (made by Toho), and Magnifica (from Mill Hill). They are consistent in size and shape with thin walls and large holes. You'll find them in an impressively wide range of colors and in sizes 15°, 11°, 10°, and 8°. Aiko size 11°s run slightly larger than Delica size 11°s and are not perfectly interchangeable. Choose cylinder beads when your design requires precisely and consistently sized beads.

Charlottes, true cuts, and one cuts are seed beads with a single facet. This cut edge catches light, creating a sparkly look. Charlottes and true cuts are made in the Czech Republic. Although you'll hear these three terms frequently interchanged, technically, a charlotte is a size 13° single-faceted bead and true cut describes all other sizes of single-faceted Czech seed beads. Japanese beads shaped like this are commonly called one cuts (and thus beads with three facets are called three cuts).

charlottes

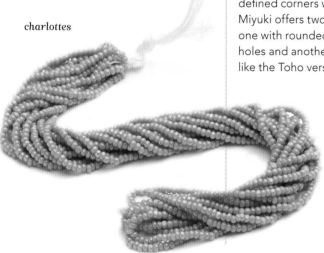

Japanese seed beads share characteristics of both Czech seed beads (because they are donutlike and round) and cylinder beads (because they are more consistently sized than Czech seed beads). Thanks to more consistent sizing, you'll spend less time culling these beads.

hex cuts

Hex cuts have six evenly spaced, equal-sized surfaces that reflect light, resulting in a shiny bead. Hex cuts (and other shapes such as bugles, triangles, and cubes) are extruded as shaped beads, whereas faceted beads (such as charlottes) are cut by running strands of seed beads against a grinding tool.

triangles

Triangles have three distinct sides. Those made by Toho have sharply defined corners with triangular holes. Miyuki offers two style of triangles, one with rounded corners with round holes and another with sharp corners like the Toho version.

Bugle beads are long tubes of glass. Bugles that range from 2mm to 11mm long are referred to by size, but be careful when you shop because Czech bugles and Japanese bugles are labeled differently (for example, a Czech size 1 is 2mm; a Japanese size 1 is 3mm); longer beads are sold by length, up to 35mm. To prevent thread breakage sometimes caused by the sharp ends of these beads, string one seed bead before and after each bugle, treating the three beads as one. Look for twisted and spiral bugle beads for added sparkle.

cubes

Cubes have four distinct sides and usually relatively large holes.

drops

Drops (also called teardrops, magatamas, and fringe beads) are 2.8mm to 6mm teardrop-shaped beads with one hole and a bulbous end. Though you'll find these terms used interchangeably, Miyuki's magatamas are a little different than other drops: They have a less pronounced teardrop shape, a nearly round front profile, and an oval side profile, and are currently available in 2.8mm and 3.4mm. Miyuki's long magatamas are 4x7mm and come to a gentle point at the end.

peanut-shaped

matte finish

dyed

permanent
galvanized

Peanut-shaped beads, as their name suggests, are shaped like peanuts and have one hole in the center. They are distributed by Matsuno as "peanut beads," those imported directly from the Czech Republic are called *farfalle* (Italian for butterflies), and Miyuki's version is called "berry beads."

seed bead finishes

The finishes added to beads drastically affect their color, often making the process of choosing colors complex. For example, a shiny red bead is no longer just red when treated with an AB (aurora borealis) coating. Thus, it's important to stitch a small sample to see how your beads will complement each other before diving into a large project. Plus, the way a bead looks inside its tube (or strung on a hank thread) can be drastically different from the way it will look when standing on its own. And it's not just about color—the balance of shiny and matte should also be a large consideration when selecting beads for a project.

aurora borealis
or iris finish

AB (aurora borealis) and iris finishes give the bead surface a rainbow, somewhat oily-looking effect. This coating is quite stable compared to dyed and galvanized coatings.

Matte seeds beads have a frosted appearance.

color-lined and
silver-lined

Hold a **color-lined/silver-lined** bead up to the light and you may find the bead to be a different color than you expected. A bead that looks solid green on your bead mat may actually be amber with a green lining. Beads with silver or gold linings have extra sparkle.

luster
finish

Luster is a general term for a shiny, glassy seed bead without special AB coating, matte finishing, or lining.

transparent

opaque

Opaque beads are solidly colored and do not allow light to pass through them.

Transparent beads are primarily clear with a touch of color.

Beware of **dyed** and **galvanized** beads because their finishes may wear off. Look for permanent galvanized and Duracoat beads and ask your bead vendor about the coating's durability. Otherwise, after wearing your jewelry a few times, you may end up with a design made of only white or silver beads. Some beaders finish their work with clear floor polish (such as Pledge Floor Finish with Future Shine) or clear acrylic spray to protect the coatings, but, if you choose this route, go lightly so you don't end up with a sticky piece of jewelry.

fancy
stones

chatons

rivolis

rivolis, fancy stones, and chatons

A **rivoli** is a holeless round crystal faceted to a point on both the front and the back. **Chatons** are flat on the front, faceted to a point on the back, and typically smaller (1.3mm to 12mm) than rivolis. Holeless, faceted crystals found in shapes other than round are referred to as **fancy stones**. All are commonly available with a foil backing added to enhance the color and sparkle of the crystal. To incorporate these holeless elements into jewelry designs, beadweavers use seed beads to create bezels that surround the outside edges and sometimes the backs.

cabochons

fire-polished

freshwater pearls

cabochons

Often called a "cab," a **cabochon** is a flat or domed glass, stone, plastic, ceramic, crystal, etc., element with a flat bottom and no holes. They are most commonly glued to a beading foundation and beaded around or bezeled with seed beads.

crystals

crystals

Crystals come in various sizes, shapes, and colors and are almost always faceted. Use beading wire or braided beading thread when stringing crystals because the sharp edges of the holes in the beads may cut through nylon beading thread. The two most popular manufacturers of these leaded glass beads are the Austrian company Swarovski and the Czech company Preciosa.

other glass

Fire-polished beads are glass beads (generally from the Czech Republic) that are faceted to catch light and often have a surface finish applied to them for extra sparkle. Because of the large number of facets, fire-polished rounds tend to be slightly oval in shape. Fire-polished beads are an affordable alternative to crystals.

pressed glass

Pressed-glass beads (also generally from the Czech Republic) are made by pressing glass into molds. They come in a variety of colors, sizes, and shapes, including rounds, flowers, leaves, and more.

lampwork

Lampwork beads are artisan-made beads created by working hot glass rods over a flame (in the old days, a lamp; today, a propane torch).

pearls

Freshwater pearls are cultured in inland lakes and rivers. These are genuine pearls cultivated by inserting irritants into farmed mussels to stimulate their production; nacre coating is formed around these irritants, resulting in unevenly sized pearls. Freshwater pearls are offered in innumerable sizes, shapes, and colors.

crystal pearls

Crystal pearls are imitation pearls made by Swarovski and others and have a crystal core coated with a thick pearl-like substance. They are perfectly shaped and have a weight similar to that of genuine pearls. And unlike freshwater pearls, they have uniform holes.

stones

stones

Stones are available in a wide range of colors, sizes, cuts, and qualities. The holes can be tiny and require a small (size 13 or 15) beading needle. If the edges are sharp, be sure to use a durable thread such as FireLine. Because it's common for lower-priced stones to have inconsistently drilled holes, I often buy twice as many strands as I think I might need. Or, try adjusting the holes yourself with a bead reamer.

← thermally bonded thread

↑ braided beading threads

↑ nylon beading thread

thread wax and conditioner →

FINDINGS

beading thread

Regardless of which type of thread you prefer, always be sure to choose a color that closely matches your beads. Your beads are meant to be the star of your project, and thread is merely the underlying structure. If you're ever unhappy with the color of exposed threads, you can try coloring them with a fine-point permanent marker.

Braided beading thread is a highly durable synthetic thread made of many fine strands braided together. Brands include PowerPro, Berkley's FireLine, Beadalon's DandyLine, and The BeadSmith's Spiderwire. Many were first designed for the fishing industry, so you'll often see them sized in terms of "pounds test" (meaning the number of pounds of pressure a single thread can withstand before breaking). The lower the pound test, the thinner the thread. Many beaders find 6 lb test to be suitable for most beadweaving

projects. If your project requires many passes through size 15° beads, consider using 4 lb test. Because of its resistance to fraying and strength, this thread is a great choice for beading crystals. Another nice feature is that it doesn't stretch. Most brands are only manufactured in two to three colors—smoke, crystal (white), and bright green.

WildFire by Beadalon is a durable, **thermally bonded beading thread** with no stretch. Available in two sizes, .006" and .008", this thread will not fray and cannot be pierced with a needle. I've found pieces made with this thread to be a bit stiff, making it a great choice for beaded ropes or other pieces of beadwork that you want to hold their shape.

Nymo and C-Lon **nylon beading threads** are available in a wide range of colors, making it easy to ensure the color of your thread always blends in with your beads. These threads are also available in several sizes—ranging from OOO (very fine) to G (the heaviest), with sizes OO, O, and

A–F in between. Nylon thread does have a tendency to stretch over time, so it's always a good idea to give the thread a little pull to remove the stretch before making your project. Be sure to protect against fraying with thread wax or conditioner. The fewer passes a thread has through beads, the less it is likely to fray, so consider using shorter lengths of this type of thread. Also made of nylon, One-G is a strong thread manufactured by Toho. In my experience, it is less likely to fray than other nylon threads. Its size is similar to Nymo B.

thread wax and conditioner

Beeswax, microcrystalline wax, and **thread conditioner** (Thread Heaven) are all used to protect your thread from wear and tear. They can also help prevent tangling, especially when working with nylon thread. Microcrystalline wax seems to be a favorite among beaders because it goes on lightly, doesn't ball up, and isn't sticky (like beeswax can be). To apply any of these thread protectors, sandwich the thread between the wax/conditioner and your index finger and thumb and pull the thread. If desired, repeat once or twice more. When applying additional coats, it's a good idea to run the thread between your fingers to smooth out any excess wax/conditioner. If working with nylon thread, you can also prestretch it at this stage. Wax/condition your thread if your project calls for a long thread that passes through beads many times or through rough- or sharp-edged beads such as crystals. And if you have trouble holding tight tension, waxing/conditioning is a must. For other projects, it's a matter of preference.

beading wire

beading wire

This wire is a strong, flexible stringing material made of multiple thin wires (usually steel) that have been coated with nylon. The more strands of wires used, the more flexible the beading wire is. This wire is most commonly secured with crimp tubes and crimp beads. Sizes .014 and .015 are great for lighter projects and best used with 1mm or 1x2mm crimp tubes and micro crimping pliers (see more on crimping pliers on page 17). Sizes .018 and .019 are great for medium-weight to heavy projects; use with 2mm crimp tubes. Be sure to check the wire manufacturer's size recommendations when pairing wire with crimp tubes.

bead stops

Bead stops are springlike or cliplike findings that temporarily snap onto the end of beading wire to prevent spills while stringing. The smaller versions can be used in the same manner on beading thread to replace the need for stop/tension beads.

crimp
cover ↓

crimp
tube ↓

← crimp bead

crimp findings

A **crimp tube** is a small cylinder of metal (most often sterling silver, gold-filled, brass, or copper) that is manipulated with wire crimping pliers to secure beading wire to a finding. See page 161 for how-to.

A **crimp cover** is a hollow, partially opened C-shaped bead that wraps around a crimp tube or bead to conceal it, giving jewelry a clean finishing touch.

metal
wire

metal wire

Hard, half-hard, and **dead-soft** are terms that refer to the "temper" (hardness or softness) of the wire. Half-hard is most commonly used for creating wrapped-loop links and dangles. If you have just one temper in your bead stash, make it half-hard because it is flexible yet strong. Wire is naturally "work hardened" through manipulation; if overworked, the wire will become brittle and break.

Craft wire is copper wire that has been permanently coated with a colored finish. This wire tends to be soft and the color coating can chip, so use light pressure or work with nylon-coated pliers or pliers covered in painter's tape to minimize marring the wire.

Gauge is used to indicate the thickness of the wire. The most versatile wire sizes for making simple wrapped loops and links are 22- and 24-gauge. Use a thicker wire (the lower the number, the thicker the wire) if making your own clasp hooks.

metal finishes

metal finishes

Gold-filled beads and findings are made of base metal (an inexpensive, nonprecious metal) that is bonded with a layer of gold that must be at least 10k gold and equal to at least $\frac{1}{20}$ of the whole piece's weight.

Gold-plated materials are bonded with a layer of gold that must be at least 10k—the same requirement as gold filled. The difference is that the layer need not be $\frac{1}{20}$ of the piece's weight; it can be much thinner.

Silver-plated refers to a base-metal component coated with fine silver.

Sterling silver beads and findings are 92.5 percent pure silver and 7.5 percent copper. Look for the "925" designation stamp on your components and jewelry.

Brass is composed of copper and zinc. "Raw" brass describes components with a goldlike appearance, and "natural brass" components have a darker bronzelike finish. "Antique brass" is a shade somewhere in between the two but isn't necessarily vintage.

filigrees

filigrees

Filigrees are metal components, such as pendants, beads, connectors, and links, that feature lacelike ornamental openwork. They are available in numerous metals and finishes.

toggle

clasps

Toggle clasp. These clasps have a bar on one side and a ring on the other. Because the bar must pass through the ring when attaching the necklace or bracelet, be sure to string at least ½" (1.3 cm) of small beads at the end of the strand before the bar.

tube

Tube clasps. Found with either a long bar or a set of loops on each side, these tubular clasps are great for finishing beadwoven designs because of their clean profile. One half slides inside the other, and most styles have small magnets in the ends to help secure the closure. When attaching, make sure the ends will align when closed.

← box

↑ lobster

Box clasps. Shaped like a rectangle, square, or circular box on one end, these clasps have a bent metal tab on the other end that snaps into the box under its own tension. The tops often have stone, glass, pearl, filigree, or other decorative inlays, and the ends often have numerous metal loops (and sometimes jump rings) to accommodate multiple strands.

Lobster clasps. These (often small) closures open and close like a claw and are great for connecting jewelry to chain.

snaps

Snaps. Snaps are also sold as sewing notions but are great for beadweaving projects. The larger the snap, the stronger the closure. If your design calls for small snaps, try to incorporate several for added security. They are a great option if you desire a concealed, inconspicuous clasp. Sew them to beadwork just as you would to clothing, making several passes up and down through each opening. Pass through adjacent beads when possible, but, if needed, you can sew between beads, looping around threads on the beaded base. Backing each snap with a small piece of Ultrasuede will also secure their connection.

bead caps

caps and cones

Bead caps are decorative metal cup-shaped elements strung snugly against the top or bottom of a bead.

cones

Cones are cylindrical findings that taper to a point at one end. They are great for neatly gathering the ends of multiple strands or covering the end of a beaded rope. Use at least 2" (5 cm) of gauged wire and form a wrapped loop that attaches to the end of your design. Use the wire end to string the wide end of the cone to cover the ends of the strands (or rope), then form a second wrapped loop that attaches to a clasp. Large bead caps can be used in the same manner.

chains

chain

Chain is available in a multitude of finishes, sizes, and shapes, including oval, round, short-and-long, and more. Most often the links are soldered and must be cut open. However, if the links are already split (unsoldered), they can be opened and closed like jump rings and no links will be wasted. Chain is measured by the size of an individual link.

jump rings

rings

Jump rings are small, usually circular or oval pieces of wire used to connect jewelry components to each other. Most jump rings are unsoldered (called open), meaning they are severed and can be opened and closed to string components. Some are soldered (called closed), meaning they cannot be opened and closed, only linked to. When attaching beading thread to a jump ring, use a soldered ring at every possible chance to avoid the likelihood of the thread escaping the ring.

split rings

Split rings are similar to key rings: two overlapping loops of wire prevent the ring from being pulled open. Thus, they are a great choice if attaching beading thread to a ring.

TOOLS

work surface

A **bead mat** is a necessity to prevent beads from rolling off your work surface. The best are made of Vellux—consider buying a blanket and cutting it into mats for all of your beading friends!

I don't go anywhere without my **portable bead studio.** To make one, find a nice box that's at least 8" × 11" × 2" (20.5 × 28 × 5 cm), fill it with your project pattern, beads, needles, extra needles, a way to store broken needles, scissors and/or thread burner, notepad and pencil, thread wax/conditioner, bead mat, small ruler, and chain- or flat-nose pliers. You never know when you'll be called in for a long meeting or sitting in a waiting room.

A **design board** is a valuable tool that prevents beads from rolling around your work surface. Most have semicircular grooves in the shape of a necklace or bracelet that allows you to visualize a design before it is strung. Although this is not a required tool for beadweaving, you may find it very helpful when designing your own jewelry.

needles

Stock up your stash with size 10 and 12 **beading needles**—these two sizes accommodate most beading projects you'll encounter. The larger the number, the thinner the needle. Never force a needle through your beads. Instead, switch to a thinner needle, such as a size 13 or 15, when navigating tight spots, or you might break beads. It's not uncommon for thin needles to break; just be sure to safely dispose of the broken parts. Size 13 and 15 needles are also necessary when beading with most stones and freshwater pearls.

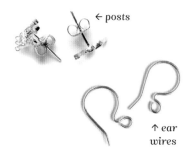

← posts

↑ ear wires

earring findings

Ear wires and **posts** are available in a number of styles and finishes. If purchasing posts, remember that the backs (or "ear nuts") are often sold separately.

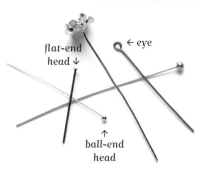

flat-end head ↓

← eye

↑ ball-end head

pins

A **flat-end head pin** is the most common style of head pin. When a bead is strung on one, the flat end sits flush against the hole in the bead. If the gauge is not indicated, it is probably 24-gauge; this gauge is strong yet thin enough to accommodate most beads. Head pins are often used to wire-wrap a dangle to a piece of jewelry. A **ball-end head pin** has a round, instead of flat, end. **Eye pins** work like head pins, but have a simple loop at one end so that they may be connected to other design elements.

beading mat

←triangle

↓ thread burner

←scissors

needles ↓

John James
Sharps
Long...

John James
Sharps
Longues
Nähnadeln lang
L4310

thread ↗ bobbin

↑ rubber needle puller

Sharps measure about 1" (2.5 cm) long (much shorter than the standard 2" or 5 cm long beading needles) and therefore can be hard to hold when stitching. However, they can be very useful when stitching in tight spots.

Rubber needle pullers are small (1" or 2.5 cm) discs of textured rubber—much like what you use to open tightly lidded jars in the kitchen—that can help you get a grip on the needle. Look for these at your needlework or craft store.

thread bobbin

To help control a long tail thread while stitching or to keep an in-progress project's thread from tangling during storage and transportation, wrap it around a **No-Tangle** bobbin. The snap-down side will keep the thread from raveling.

triangles

A small metal **triangle** is a simple yet valuable tool for quickly cleaning your bead mat. It is the perfect scoop for picking up beads, and the pointed corners make it easy to sort beads and pour them back into their tubes. You can also pour your beads back into the tubes by using a rolled up conical piece of paper that acts like a funnel.

bead storage

How you choose to store your beads comes down to personal preference. I have a rolling cabinet with several drawers that hold my seed beads sorted by color. Some beaders sort by bead type, others sort by size. You may prefer clear plastic tackle, thread storage, or hardware storage boxes (check the needlework, fishing, and tool departments at your local stores). They allow you to see your

beads without cracking open the lid and are easy to transport. Plus, the caps on seed bead tubes can pop off, making solid boxes where the tubes won't slide around or get crushed ideal. When you store hanks, tie a knot around the last bead on the hank thread to prevent the rest of the beads from sliding off.

cutting tools

Be sure to keep your **scissors** sharp. The cleaner the cut on the end of the thread, the easier it will be to thread your needle. Interestingly, children's Fiskars scissors are great at making a clean edge when cutting braided beading threads such as FireLine.

A **thread burner** is great for cutting threads close to beads. Not only does this tool let you get in close to the beads, making sure no little thread tail is showing, but it also lightly melts the end of synthetic threads, creating a ball that keeps the final knot from coming untied. Don't use a thread burner when cutting thread off the spool, otherwise the small ball of melted thread will make threading the needle difficult. Here's a tip: When you're ready to end a thread, knot it, weave through a few beads, and "cut" the thread with the thread burner 1/16" (2 mm) away from the last bead exited. Then chase the tiny tail to the base of the beadwork, melting it and encouraging it to ball up.

Wire cutters (or **flush cutters**) are used to cut both gauged wire and beading wire. Their sharp edges ensure that no burrs are left on the trimmed ends of the wire.

pliers

The inside jaws of both **chain-** and **flat-nose** pliers are flat and smooth. However, the outside edges of chain-nose pliers are round on the top and bottom, and flat-nose pliers are flat on both edges. Chain-nose pliers taper toward the tip, making

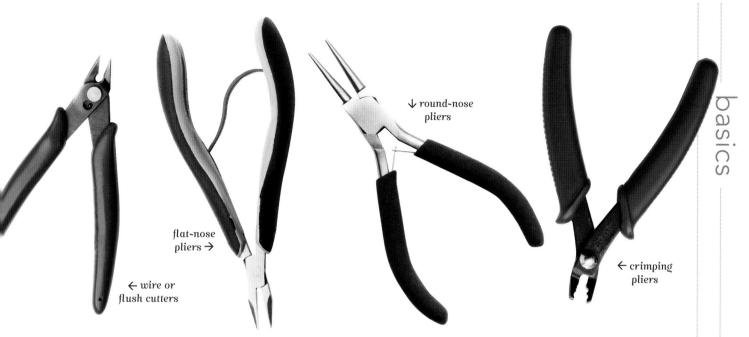

flat-nose
pliers →

← wire or
flush cutters

↓ round-nose
pliers

← crimping
pliers

them great for working with small findings and in tight spaces; flat-nose pliers are wider, giving you more gripping power. Projects that direct you to open and close jump rings will require two pairs of chain- or flat-nose pliers.

Use either to help gently push, pull, and/or wiggle your needle through tight spaces. Just make sure you aren't using the pliers to pull so hard that you break a bead; remember, it's best to switch to a smaller needle to ease stitching.

A pair of pliers is also handy if you notice a stitching error caused by adding too many seed beads. See Correcting Errors (page 20) for more information.

Round-nose pliers are used to make loops and curls with wire. Their conical jaws taper toward the tip, creating many loop-size options. If a large loop is desired, position the wire near the base of the jaw; for small loops, work the wire at the tips.

Crimping pliers have two notches and are used to secure crimp tubes on beading wire: one notch is used to flatten crimp tubes and the other is used to fold the tube in half. They are available in three sizes; pliers that accommodate 2mm tubes are the most common.

design tools

A quick Internet search for **herringbone graph paper** will yield many options for free downloadable patterned paper for designing in flat herringbone stitch. Simply print the graph paper, color in a design, and follow the chart bead by bead as you stitch **(fig. 1)**.

To help mark your stitching progress, photocopy the pattern and cross out rows as you work. Or, place the pattern in a clear plastic sheet protector and black out the completed sections with a permanent marker. You can also track progress directly on the pattern with a pencil and erase the marks when done.

Photocopiers are great for testing the scale and overall look of any design. This tool was invaluable when designing my Graceful Garland necklace (page 58). After beading just one flower, I made several photocopies of it. I then cut the paper copies out and played around with several ways to arrange them. Finally, I taped them all together to determine the overall length and started beading the rest of the project. This is one of my favorite ways to design.

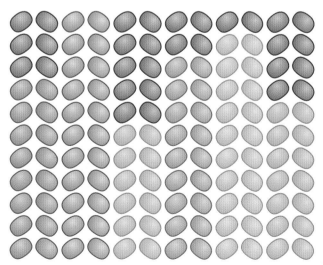

fig. 1

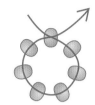

fig. 2

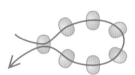

fig. 3

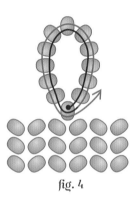

fig. 4

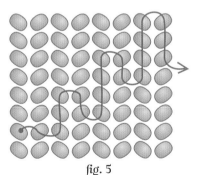

fig. 5

MUST-KNOW TERMS

Column, also referred to as a "stack," "ladder," or "spine," is a vertical two-bead-wide line of angled beads that forms after working several rows/rounds of herringbone stitch. See page 25 for a diagram and more information.

Conditioned vs **waxed thread.** Conditioned thread is lightly coated with a synthetic thread conditioner, usually Thread Heaven (in the little blue box). Waxed thread is treated with beeswax or microcrystalline wax.

Cull your beads. Remove beads that are wider or skinnier than the average-size bead—using consistently sized beads results in uniform beadwork.

To **pass through** means to pass through a bead a second time, moving the needle (or wire) in the same direction as the first pass **(fig. 2)**.

To **pass back through,** move the needle (or wire) in the opposite direction as the first pass **(fig. 3)**.

Repeat. When the word **repeat** appears after a semicolon, repeat the instructions that precede it in that sentence only. For example, here you'll work the entire sequence three times for a grand total of 6 stitches: "Work 1 herringbone stitch with 2A and 1 herringbone stitch with 2B; repeat twice."

Repeat from *. Repeat the instructions, starting at the text that immediately follows the *.

Repeat the thread path to reinforce. Retrace the previous thread path to strengthen the row/round/loop **(fig. 4)**. You may need to weave through beads and work a turnaround before you are in position to retrace the thread path.

Row vs **round.** Rows of herringbone stitch are worked back and forth; rounds are worked in a circle.

Secure the thread and trim. Tie 1 or 2 knots around threads between nearby beads, weave through 3 or 4 beads, and trim the tail close to the beadwork with scissors or a thread burner. (See Starting and Ending Threads on page 19 for more information on forming knots.)

Step up. Use a step-up to prepare for the next row (or round). Unless otherwise directed, do this by exiting the first bead added in the current row/round.

Stitch. When directed to work a herringbone stitch, string 2 beads, pass through the next bead of the current column, and up through the first bead of the next column. This entire sequence is considered 1 stitch.

String 1A (or 1B, 1C, etc.). Use a needle to pick up one of the beads designated A (or B, C, etc.) in the materials list and slide it onto the thread.

String {1A and 2B} three times. Repeat the entire sequence inside the brackets three times. In this example, the strand would begin with 1A, 2B, 1A, 2B, etc. (not 3A and 6B).

Turnaround. Change the direction of beading without exposing the thread or deviating from the established thread path. Techniques for turning around at the end of flat-herringbone rows begin on page 25.

Weave through beads. Pass your needle through beads until you exit the bead indicated in the pattern. Take the path that leaves no exposed threads and don't make any moves that might tweak the beadwork by pulling a bead in an undesired direction **(fig. 5)**.

Working thread. The working thread is the end with the needle, doing the work of stitching. The opposite end is the **tail thread.**

BEADING 101

stringing

When **stringing,** simply use a needle and thread or wire (beading or gauged) to pick up beads and gather them into a strand **(fig. 6)**.

threading the needle

Instead of holding your needle out in front of you and passing the thread through the eye, think of "needling the thread." To do so, hold the thread between the thumb and index finger of your nondominant hand with the thread just barely sticking out, just ¹⁄₁₆" (2 mm) or so. Use your other hand to slide the eye of the needle down over the tip of the thread **(fig. 7)**.

Slide the needle down the thread so about one-third of the thread folds back onto itself. As you work, move the needle down the length of the thread as needed to control the amount of working thread.

starting and ending threads

When starting a new project, leave a 6" (15 cm) tail so you have something to hold on to when working the first few rounds or rows. Sometimes a project will call for you to leave a longer tail to use during a later step; don't trim until indicated.

Some beaders like to add a **stop bead** in a contrasting color before the first beads strung **(fig. 8)**. This bead prevents beads from sliding off the thread. Although a stop bead is also sometimes called a "tension

bead," it usually slides around too much to offer any tension control. To lessen its tendency to slide around, pass through the stop bead twice; avoid splitting the thread of the first pass. Be sure to remove the stop bead before completing your project.

To **end a thread,** make an overhand knot over a previous thread: Exit the bead closest to where you want the knot, pass the needle under the nearest thread of a previous row (or round) from back to front. Pull the thread to form a ¼" (6 mm) loop and pass through the loop from back to front **(fig. 9)**. Pull to secure the knot. Weave through a few more beads before trimming. If desired, tie a second knot and weave through more beads before trimming for extra security. Never trim the thread next to the knot—it will always find a way to come undone. *Note:* When ending a thread and adding a new one, be sure to follow the previous thread path, otherwise you may distort the work and the angle of the herringbone beads.

To **add a new thread mid-project,** pass the needle with the new thread under a previous thread a few stitches away from where you want to resume beading, leaving a 4" (10 cm) tail. Tie 2 overhand knots around the previous thread and weave through beads to pick up where you left off. Add a needle to the new thread's tail and weave it through beads before trimming the thread **(fig. 10,** new thread in red; old thread in blue). If you know it will be hard to tell where you left off (such as when working a spiral tubular rope), consider adding the new thread before ending the old thread. To hide any knot, tug the thread to pull the knot inside a bead. However, only do this if you know you won't need to pass through the bead again later.

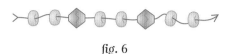

fig. 6

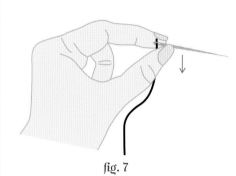

fig. 7

fig. 8

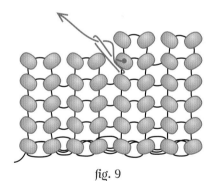

fig. 9

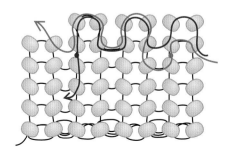

fig. 10

To avoid having to later weave the tail thread through the work, try this trick: Pass the new thread through a few beads, tie a half-hitch knot around a previous thread, and weave through a few more beads until you reach the bead you want to exit. Then, pull back on the tail thread to remove any slack and trim.

Here's a great technique I picked up from Melanie Potter. Once 6" to 8" (15 to 20.5 cm) of working thread remains, attach a new thread to the old thread before tying off the working thread. This saves thread and helps you keep your place. To do this, tie a slipknot (see page 162 for how-to) 6" to 8" (15 to 20.5 cm) from the end of the tail of the new thread, pass the remaining working thread through the slipknot, and pull the slipknot until it's closed, but not so tight that it can't slide along the working thread. Before tightening the slipknot all the way, pull the old and new working threads to slide the slipknot down to meet the beadwork. Now tighten the slipknot, then weave in and trim the old and new tails.

single thread vs doubled thread

Unless otherwise directed, work your project using a **single thread.** If you are using a durable thread and seed beads without sharp holes, a single thread is usually sufficient.

Using a **doubled thread** is great when working with large-holed beads. Using more thread fills the bead holes more quickly, and beads that have more thread hold tighter tension because they don't slide around as much. Doubled thread is also nice when working with crystals because the second thread acts as a backup in the event a sharp crystal edge cuts the first thread. Doubled thread is also great in sections of beadwork that benefit from

reinforcement, such as when joining the ends of two pieces of beadwork or forming a loop of beads that connects a clasp.

To double the thread at the start of a project, begin with a thread that is twice as long as what you are used to working with, slide your needle to the center, and join the ends to double the thread.

Or try this great method I picked up from Cynthia Rutledge: Start with a thread that is twice as long as what you are used to working with, work a few stitches, and then slide the needle toward the starting end of the thread so the tail extends a few inches beyond the last bead added. The thread is now doubled. This method is ideal when you want to double a thread mid-project **(fig. 11).**

Regardless of how you doubled the thread, you may have to slide your needle back to the center of the thread several times during the course of a project. If you need to undo any incorrect stitches, you may need to cut the fold and remove the needle. To add the needle back on, you'll have to fit both threads through the same eye.

clockwise vs counterclockwise

Most right-handed beaders prefer to work circular herringbone counterclockwise. When looking down at the top round of a rope, they work tubular herringbone clockwise. Thus, the majority of illustrations in this book are presented in this manner. If you're left-handed or just prefer to stitch in the other direction, work each round accordingly. Keep in mind that if you change the direction of stitching for twists and spirals, your beadwork will twist/spiral in the opposite direction.

tangles and knots

To help avoid pesky **tangles,** keep your thread waxed or conditioned. If you notice your thread starting to twist, hold up the beadwork and allow the needle and thread to dangle and untwist. Stretching nylon thread after waxing/conditioning it can sometimes help avoid tangles. If a thread just won't stop tangling, end that thread and start a new one; the first may just be too worn, or static may be causing the problem.

Treat **knots** as you would tangles—wax/condition your thread as a preventive measure, and if all else fails, end that thread and start a new one. Once you see a knot start to form, use the tip of your needle to try to undo it before it gets too tight.

correcting errors

If you make an error, fix it. You may be discouraged once you find a mistake, but you'll be much happier in the long run if you go back to correct it. Make light of the situation by thinking of it as the "frog stitch"— Rip it! Rip it!

When dealing with an **incorrect bead count,** it's often easy to remove an extra bead. Instead of tearing out the beadwork until you reach the misplaced bead (size 10° or smaller), carefully break it using the tip of chain-nose pliers. To do so, use the pliers to grip the bead you want to break, hold the piece down and away from you, and squeeze hard to break the bead. It's best to do this outside while wearing safety glasses. Beware that the process of breaking the bead may cut or damage your thread. Plus, the stitch that once held the bead may be loose; stitch back through beads to lessen the slack and reinforce the stitch. If you accidentally forgot a bead, it's best to rip out what you've done to correct the problematic stitch.

If you have a **broken bead,** first make sure that all small parts of the broken bead have been removed. You have two choices: 1) rip out what you've done and replace the broken bead with a new one, or 2) stitch a new bead in the empty spot created by the broken bead. If choosing the latter, be sure to repeat all of the thread paths around the new bead and use tight tension to pull the new bead down in place over the exposed thread left by the broken bead. The first option will give you the cleanest result, but, if a bead breaks in a spot that would be extremely difficult to undo, you can get away with the second option.

tension

Tension describes the tightness of the thread as it passes through beads. Beadwork worked with tight tension will be stiff and rigid; beadwork worked with loose tension will be flexible. Tight tension is essential when making dimensional pieces.

To achieve **tight tension,** give the thread a strong tug after each stitch. It's natural for previously placed stitches to loosen as you work across a row (or round), so give the thread an extra pull at the end of each row or round before starting the next. Pull up on the herringbone pairs as needed. Waxed or conditioned thread will be slightly sticky and will help set tension. You can also set tension by tying an inconspicuous knot.

Sometimes **looser tension** is needed, but never use tension so loose that thread is left exposed between beads or that a bead hangs from the beadwork. Think of it as relaxed tension—don't give the thread a hard tug after working each stitch. If a finished piece of beadwork is too rigid, then a slight squeeze can break beads.

I naturally bead with tight tension, so when a lighter tension is needed, I consciously think of relaxing my hands.

joining herringbone ends

Two ends of herringbone stitch can be joined by following a herringbone thread path **(fig. 12).** The cleanest joins are made when the starting end wasn't formed with a ladder stitch, but was made with a stacked start instead (see page 26 for how to do this).

zipping peyote ends

Two edges of peyote stitch can be "zipped" together by passing from the up bead on one side of the beadwork to the up bead on the other side of the beadwork, interlocking the beads like teeth on a zipper. If using this method to turn a flat strip of peyote into a tube, make sure the strip is worked with an even number of rows **(fig. 13).**

tight spots

Don't get discouraged if you find yourself in a tough situation where you just can't angle the needle exactly where you want it to go. For example, if you work a beaded rope with tight tension and later want to add embellishments, the work might be too tight to offer any give when trying to angle your needle. In this situation, the needle may want to pass through more than just the one bead you intended. Go ahead and make the stitch, then simply remove the needle and pull the thread back out of the bead(s) you didn't intend to pass through.

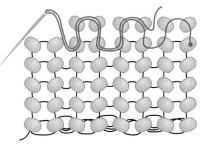

fig. 11

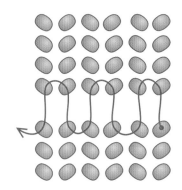

fig. 12

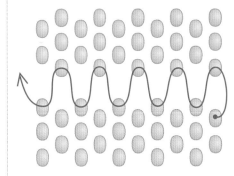

fig. 13

HERRINGBONE STITCH BASICS

Many beaders prefer to start herringbone off a ladder-stitched base. Here's what you need to know about ladder stitch:

ladder stitch

For **1-needle ladder stitch,** string 2 beads and pass through both of them again. Manipulate the beads so they sit side by side **(fig. 14, blue).** String 1 bead, then pass through the last bead added and the one just strung; repeat, adding 1 bead at a time and working in a figure-eight pattern **(fig. 14, red).**

For **2-needle ladder stitch,** add a needle to each end of the thread. String 1 bead and slide it to the center of the thread. Use 1 needle to string 1 bead, then pass the other needle back through the bead just added; repeat to form a strip **(fig. 15).**

This **quick-start ladder variation** results in a thread path identical to 2-needle ladder stitch but only requires 1 needle. Not only is this method fast, but it's also a great choice when working with small beads because it doesn't fill the bead holes with excess thread like 1-needle ladder stitch can. Begin by stringing the beads of Row 1 and pass through the second-to-last bead strung **(fig. 16).** Snug the beads so they sit side by side. Pass through the previous Row 1 bead and snug the beads again **(fig. 17);** continue in this manner until you reach the first bead of Row 1.

As the strip develops, you may want to roll the beadwork around between your fingers so you're always stitching right to left. You may also see this referred to as a variation on square stitch or as a "back-stitched ladder start." See how to use this technique for a 2-bead-high ladder in Leslie Frazier's Buena Vista necklace (page 120).

herringbone prep

If this is your first time with herringbone stitch, you may find it helpful to use large beads and a stiffer thread (such as FireLine) instead of nylon thread. Starting strips worked with nylon thread tend to be flexible and hard to hold. Wax your thread to keep the beads from sliding around.

To prepare for your first herringbone stitches, ladder-stitch an even number of beads. Orient the strip in your left fingers (if you're right-handed) so the thread exits up through the last bead added, with that last bead on the right end of the strip. Many beaders like to work with a long tail wrapped around their pinky or several fingers—find what is most comfortable for you.

Now you are ready for your first herringbone stitches.

herringbone stitch

To work Row 1 of **flat herringbone stitch,** string 2 beads, then pass down through the next bead in the ladder and up through the following bead; repeat to the end of the row. Step up for the next row by wrapping the thread around previous threads and exiting back up through the first bead of Row 1 and the last bead strung **(fig. 18, blue).** To work Row 2, string 2 beads and pass down through the next bead of the previous row in the current column and up through the following bead; repeat, stringing 2 beads per stitch and passing down, then up, through 2 beads of the previous row. Step up for the next row as before **(fig. 18, red).** The 2-bead stitch will cause the beads to angle in each column, like a herringbone fabric.

Note: Make sure the beads "pop" into place, with holes angling away from each other. If needed, pull up on the pair of beads to adjust their angle.

If you always prefer to work from right to left (as most right-handed beaders do), then flip the work in your hand after each row. There are a handful of ways to turnaround at the end of each row. See more methods starting on page 28.

Now that you know the basic structure of herringbone stitch, begin working this stitch in flat, circular, and tubular variations by exploring the following in-depth technique sections that open each chapter. Plus, learn umpteen methods for shaping and adding embellishments.

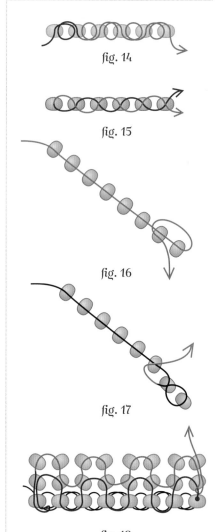

fig. 14

fig. 15

fig. 16

fig. 17

fig. 18

flat herringbone stitch

Get inspiring results by incorporating accent beads into flat herringbone stitch in the projects that follow.

A fun mix of accent beads added between each stitched column of my flat herringbone **Reflections** bracelet creates a wonderfully serpentine effect. Plus, with the variety of pressed-glass and seed beads built right into each row, the embellished bracelet components are quick to stitch. Also see my variation on the design, **Timeless Cuff**.

Whether you're new to herringbone stitch or looking for a great make-it-in-a-weekend bracelet, Carole Ohl's **Chiffon Ribbon Cuff** perfectly showcases the dazzling effects that can result from basic techniques. Dress up traditional herringbone stitches with triangle beads, then add in-column crystal accents for a finishing touch. Also see my variation on the design, **Filigree Square Bracelet.**

Jean Campbell's **Jeanne Moreau** necklace is not only a show-stopping design, but its techniques are also ingenious. After adding long strands between herringbone columns, Jean goes back in to strengthen and embellish the strands, taking flat herringbone to an entirely new dimension.

TECHNIQUES

terminology

Here is the basic anatomy of a piece of flat herringbone stitch (**fig. 1**). These terms also apply when working circular and tubular variations. You may sometimes hear columns referred to as "stacks," "spines," or "ladders." Also notice the placement of the between-column and in-column accent beads; see page 29 for how to do this.

counting

Because beads don't stagger in herringbone stitch as they do in peyote stitch, counting rows is very straightforward. Simply follow a line of beads up the work: When you're working with 2 beads in each stitch, each bead you count is part of a new row (**fig. 2**). When you're working with 4 beads in each stitch, each row is 2 beads high (**fig. 3**). If the first/foundation row was worked in ladder stitch, that row is still considered Row 1, although herringbone stitch doesn't start until the following row.

In this book, and in the majority of other publications, each column is 2 beads wide. However, I have seen the term *column* used for just 1 vertical line of beads (which I refer to as a "half-column"; see examples in **fig. 8**), so be sure to fully orient yourself with the pattern when working projects from other designers. Count the columns along the top edge of the work where it is easy to see the arced thread that joins the beads (**fig. 4**).

When counting rows with accent beads, notice how the accent beads sit lower than the beads added in that same row. Here, you can see that all of the blue beads belong to the same row, even though the blue

accent bicones seem to be parallel with the row of pink seed beads below the blue seed beads (**fig. 5**).

even-count flat herringbone

It's easiest to learn the basics of flat herringbone stitch by starting with an even number of beads in each row.

LADDER START

One of the easiest ways to get started with flat herringbone is with an even-count strip of ladder stitch because it positions all of the bead holes pointing upward. See page 22 for several variations on ladder stitch. Working the ladder-stitched strip with relaxed tension will encourage the beads to angle like the herringbone stitches of the rows that follow. Many beaders prefer to work flat herringbone right to left, so position the ladder-stitched strip with the thread exiting the top of the last bead added.

BEGIN HERRINGBONE STITCH

String 2 beads, pass down through the next-to-last ladder-stitched bead, and up through the following ladder-stitched bead; repeat across the row (**fig. 6, blue**). For a basic thread-loop turnaround (or one of the alternates that follow), loop the thread around the thread bridge below the first two ladder-stitched beads, then pass back through the first ladder-stitched bead and the last bead added (**fig. 6, red**).

Work the next and following rows in the same manner: String 2 beads, then pass down through the next bead in the current column and up through the first bead of the following column (**fig. 7, blue**). (This is considered 1 stitch.) Always work a turnaround to pass back through the last bead added (**fig. 7, red**).

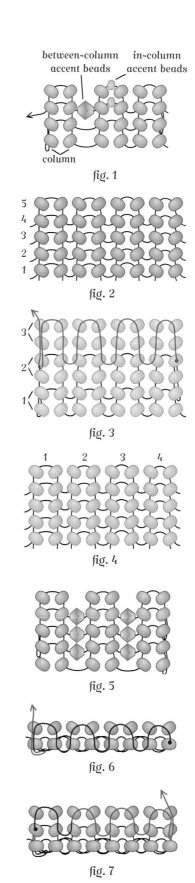

between-column accent beads   in-column accent beads

column

fig. 1

fig. 2

fig. 3

fig. 4

fig. 5

fig. 6

fig. 7

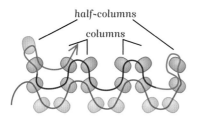

fig. 8

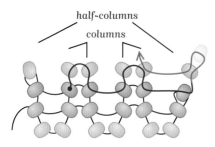

fig. 9

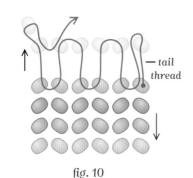

fig. 10

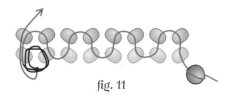

fig. 11

fig. 12

STACKED START WITH TWO HALF-COLUMNS

This technique is sometimes referred to as a "traditional start" because it can be traced back to some of the earliest herringbone-stitched artifacts; many beaders prefer it because no ladder stitch is needed. Instead, the first set of beads stack to become the beads of both Rows 1 and 2. This technique may take some time getting used to, but it's well worth the effort. Try working with 4 different colors while learning. This first variation forms 2 "half-columns" along each end of the work. Learn the technique by following this sample, then play around with your own variations:

ROWS 1 AND 2: String 1 blue bead, 2 pink beads, 2 blue beads, 2 pink beads, 2 blue beads, 2 pink beads, and 1 blue bead (**fig. 8, purple**).

ROW 3: String 1 gray bead and pass back through the final blue bead of the previous row (**Fig. 8, green**). *Note:* The final pink bead, final blue bead, and the gray bead just added are part of the half-column on this edge of the work. Skip 2 pink beads, pass up through the nearest blue bead, string 2 gray beads, and pass down through the next blue bead; repeat. Skip 2 pink beads and pass up through the following blue bead (**fig. 8, blue**). Pull back on the tail thread to encourage the beads to stack. String 1 gray bead and 1 gold bead; pass back through the gray bead just strung and up through the following gray bead (**fig. 8, red**). *Note:* The gray bead is the final bead of Row 3; the gold bead is the first bead of Row 4.

ROW 4: Work 2 herringbone stitches with 2 gold beads in each stitch (**fig. 9, blue**). String 1 gold bead and 1 green bead; pass back through the gold bead just strung and up through the following gold bead (**fig. 9, red**). *Note:* The gold bead is the final bead of Row 4; the green bead is the first bead of Row 5.

ROWS 5 AND ON: Repeat Row 4 for the desired length. At the end of the final row, don't add an extra bead (the first bead of the next row) as before. Instead, just add 1 bead (the final bead of the final row) and pass through all of the beads of the final row using a ladder-stitch thread path.

If you're not a big fan of the half-column add-ons, look what happens when you rotate the work 180° and begin stitching with the tail thread—it's just like normal herringbone!

WORKING OFF THE STARTING END

One of the most valuable things I've picked up from the "traditional start with two half-columns" technique is that it can be used to bead from the other side of a strip. Begin by working at least 5 or 6 rows of flat herringbone; leave a 3' (91.5 cm) tail thread and don't form any knots for the starting row (**fig. 10, blue arrow;** the blue arrow indicates the original direction of stitching). Be sure not to split any threads while stitching. Once you're ready to begin working off the starting end, rotate the work 180° and tear out the first couple of rows of beadwork.

Work the following rows as you did for Row 5 in the "stacked start with two half-columns" technique above (**fig. 10, red**).

STACKED START WITH TWO-BEAD COLUMNS

To begin flat herringbone stitch without the use of ladder stitch and without forming half-columns as on page 26, use square stitch at each end of the starting row. Learn the technique by following this method, then play around with your own variations:

ROWS 1 AND 2: Add a stop bead 6" (15 cm) from the end of the thread. String 1 pink bead. String {2 blue beads and 2 pink beads} three times. String 2 blue beads and 1 pink bead (**fig. 11, green**). Pass through the fourth-to-last bead added and the last bead added twice to square-stitch them together. Tie a half-hitch knot around the threads below the 2 beads (**fig. 11, blue**). Pass back through the 2 end beads (the last bead added and the second-to-last bead added) to step up for the next row (**fig. 11, red**).

ROW 3: String 2 gold beads, pass down through the next blue bead, skip 2 pink beads, and pass up through the next blue bead; repeat twice. String 2 gold beads; pass down through the next blue bead and pink bead (**fig. 12, blue**). Remove the stop bead and pull back on the tail thread to encourage the beads to stack. Square-stitch the first 2 pink beads together. Tie a half-hitch knot around the threads below the 2 pink beads and weave back through the edge beads to exit the last gold bead added (**fig. 12, red**).

ROWS 4 AND ON: Continue in flat herringbone with 2 beads in each stitch.

odd-count flat herringbone

With the help of a unique turn on one end, flat herringbone can be worked side to side with an odd number of beads. Whether starting with a strip of ladder stitch or using the stacked start method, your beadwork will have 1 half-column along one side.

LADDER START WITH ONE HALF-COLUMN

Begin by ladder-stitching an odd number of beads and position the strip with the thread exiting the top of the last bead added. Work flat herringbone stitch across the strip with 2 beads in each stitch until you reach the final bead (**fig. 13, blue**). String 2 beads, then pass back through the first bead added and up through the next bead (**fig. 13, red**). Pull the thread tight so the last 2 beads strung stack on top of each other. Notice that the first bead just added is the final bead of the current row; the last bead added is the first bead of the next row.

Continue flat herringbone stitch across the row as usual with 2 beads in each stitch. At the end of the row, work a loop-thread turnaround (or other turnaround method of your choice; see page 28 for alternatives). Work the next row as before. One edge of the work will always have the half-column turnaround; the other will always have a loop-thread (or similar) turnaround.

STACKED START WITH ONE HALF-COLUMN

In this variation, omit the ladder-stitch start and the first set of beads strung from both Rows 1 and 2. Learn the technique by following this sample, then play around with your own variations:

ROWS 1 AND 2: String 1 blue bead and 1 pink bead; pass back through the blue bead. String 1 blue bead. String {2 pink beads and 2 blue beads} twice. String 2 pink beads and 1 blue bead (**fig. 14, green**).

ROW 3: String 1 gray bead and pass back through the final blue bead of the previous row (**fig. 14, blue**). *Note:* The final pink bead, final blue bead, and the gray bead just added are part of the half-column on this edge of the work. Skip 2 pink beads and pass up through the nearest blue bead. String 2 gray beads, pass down through the next blue bead, skip 2 pink beads, and pass up through the following blue bead; repeat. String 2 gray beads and work a thread-loop turnaround to exit back through the last bead added (**fig. 14, red**). Pull back on the tail thread to encourage the beads to stack. If desired, secure the tail thread and trim it at this point to help hold the starting rows in place.

ROWS 4 AND ON: Work flat herringbone stitch with 2 beads in each stitch across the row,

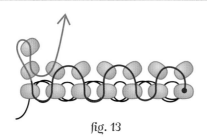

fig. 13

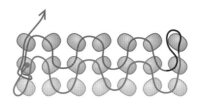

fig. 14

27

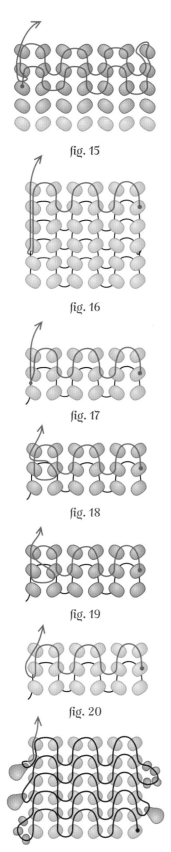

fig. 15

fig. 16

fig. 17

fig. 18

fig. 19

fig. 20

fig. 21

adding a single bead along the right edge as before to form the half-column and working the thread-loop turnaround along the left edge (**fig. 15**).

alternate turnarounds

Whether you're working even- or odd-count flat herringbone, there are several ways to turn the thread at the end of a row. See the basic thread-loop turnaround in **fig. 6** and **fig. 7** (page 25).

DEEPER THREAD-LOOP TURNAROUND

If the row previous to the one just worked is still a bit loose, considering weaving down through several edge beads before working a thread-loop turnaround (**fig. 16**). This way you're wrapping the thread around rows that feel more securely set. Just remember that this will fill your beads up with thread, which may prevent you from being able to add a clasp or other embellishments along the edge. Switch to a smaller needle any time you have trouble passing through beads.

KNOTTED TURNAROUND

If your thread-loop turnarounds come undone by slipping up through the bead above the turn-around point (this can happen if you work with tight tension), try a knotted turnaround instead. To do so, tie a small half-hitch knot in the place you'd usually work a thread loop (**fig. 17**). If the knot slips up into the bead above it after pulling the knot tight, making it hard to pass the needle back through the bead, consider passing up through the bead before fully tightening the knot. Keep in mind that the knots can fill the bead holes if you plan to pass through all of the edge beads again later.

CROSSOVER TURNAROUNDS

If you pull the thread too tight when working either of these turnarounds, you can affect the angle of the beads and disrupt the herringbone pattern, but they are a nice way to avoid loops and knots.

In the first method, after working the final stitch, pass up through the second-from-the-edge bead in the previous row. Then, pass up through the last bead strung (**fig. 18**).

Alternatively, after stringing the final 2 beads of the row, pass down through the second-from-the-edge bead in the previous row. Then, pass up through the edge bead of the previous row and the last bead strung (**fig. 19**).

EXPOSED-THREAD TURNAROUND

In all of the previous turnaround methods the thread remains hidden inside the beads. However, this quick-and-easy turnaround leaves thread exposed on the outside edges of the end beads. If you plan to later embellish the edges, or if your thread perfectly matches your beads and you don't mind the exposed thread, then give this method a try. After working the final stitch, pass back through the last bead of the current row, looping the thread around the edge bead of the previous row (**fig. 20**).

DECORATIVE TURNAROUNDS

Use the exposed-thread turnaround method to add some decoration along the edges: Simply string 1 or more beads before passing back through the last bead added (**fig. 21, blue**). Or, after stringing the decorative turnaround bead, pass back up through the last bead exited and the last bead added

Accent Beads

Slightly pull up on any herringbone stitch and notice how the threads between rows could easily be decorated with other beads. Now pull columns away from each other and notice that accent beads could fit there as well. Use the following techniques to transform your flat herringbone stitches.

IN-COLUMN ACCENTS

As the name implies, this method adds accent beads within columns of herringbone stitch, sandwiched between rows. To embellish your work in this manner, string your accent bead before the herringbone pair. After stringing the herringbone pair, pass back through the accent bead, through the next bead in the same column, and up through the first bead of the following column. Repeat this technique across the row. Be sure to step up through the last bead added as usual **(fig. A)**. Work the following row(s) in flat herringbone stitch using tight tension to snug the herringbone beads above the accent beads. At the end of the row, you might find the turnaround to be sturdier if made below the accent bead **(fig. B)**.

BETWEEN-COLUMN ACCENTS

In this variation, accent beads are added between columns. This is the most basic way to add accent beads. See the notes on counting on page 25 and notice how between-column accent beads sit much lower than the herringbone beads of the same row. After working a herringbone stitch, string your accent bead(s) before passing up through the first bead of the next column. Repeat across the row, adding accent beads between each column **(fig. C)**. It's a good idea to gradually increase the size of accent beads to avoid gaps.

The technique used to form sections of peyote stitch between columns (see page 56) can also be incorporated into flat herringbone stitch.

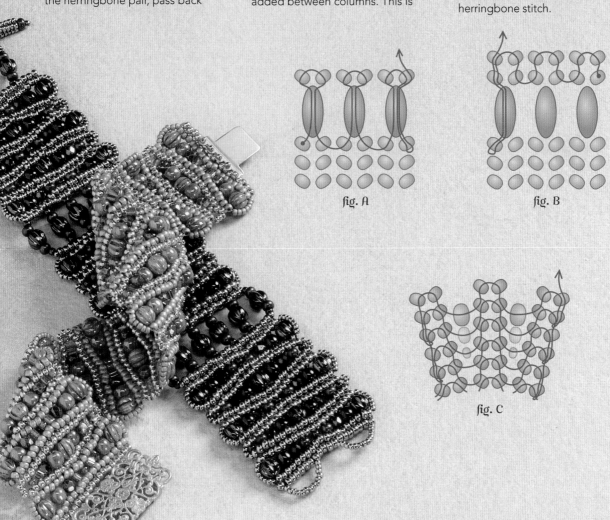

fig. A

fig. B

fig. C

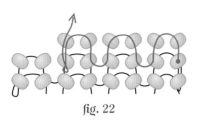

fig. 22

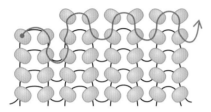

fig. 23

fig. 24

fig. 25

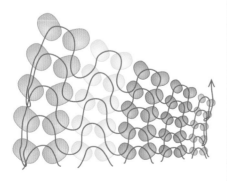

fig. 26

(fig. 21, red). Follow down one side and notice that the decorative beads sit along every other edge bead.

shaping

Whether your goal is to increase or decrease the size of your beadwork, there are countless ways to add shape. These techniques apply to circular and tubular herringbone variations as well, so experiment to find the method that works best for the project at hand.

END-ROW DECREASE

It's easy to shape the sides of flat herringbone stitch by decreasing the number of stitches in a row. If you want to work a decrease while stitching toward the end of the row, simply stop the row short and work a turnaround after the 2 beads you want to be the new edge beads **(fig. 22)**.

To decrease the work at the beginning of the row, retrace the thread path of the previous row until you're ready to start working the next herringbone row **(fig. 23)**.

END-ROW INCREASE

To increase the width of the work, ladder-stitch a strip of beads off of the last edge bead exited **(fig. 24, blue)**. Work the following row off of the ladder-stitch strip **(fig. 24, red)**. If adding an odd number of ladder-stitch beads, follow the instructions for odd-count herringbone on page 27.

BEAD SIZE AND TYPE

Play around with different sizes and types of beads and see what interesting shape changes result.

Shaping can be achieved by changing bead size from one row to the next **(fig. 25)**. Or, start the first row with a variety of beads for a curved piece of beadwork **(fig. 26)**.

MID-ROW INCREASE, BETWEEN-COLUMN

This technique and the following invaluable increase and decrease techniques were first brought to my attention by Vicki Star (www.vickistar.com) and featured in her book *Beading with Herringbone Stitch* (Interweave, 2001). To begin growing the width of the work between columns rapidly, add 2 beads between stitches just as you would add an accent bead **(fig. 27)**. In the following rows, treat the 2 new beads as the start of a new column.

For a more gradual increase, add just 1 bead between columns **(fig. 28, blue)**. In the following row, add 2 beads on top of the single increase bead, without stitching into the single increase bead **(fig. 28, red)**. From here, you have many options: 1) continue increasing the number of beads to form a strand between columns; 2) start working the sections in peyote stitch; or 3) work a new herringbone column off of this pair. See more on these three options on page 56.

MID-ROW INCREASE, IN-COLUMN

To begin growing the width of the work from within a column, work across the row as usual but include 1 stitch with 3 beads **(fig. 29)**.

In the following row, add 2 beads on each side of the middle increase bead **(fig. 30)**. In the following rows, treat these new pairs as the start of 2 new columns.

MID-ROW DECREASE, BETWEEN-COLUMN

To quickly reduce the width of your work, pass through 2 beads of the previous row without adding any beads **(fig. 31)**.

For a more gradual decrease, work just 1 bead in the decrease stitch **(fig. 32, blue)**. In the following row, skip over the single bead **(fig. 32, red)**.

MID-ROW DECREASE, IN-COLUMN

To work a decrease within a column, exit up through the first bead of a column. String 3 beads, skip over 2 beads of the previous row (the next bead of the current column and the first bead of the next column), and pass down through the next bead. Pass up through the following bead to complete the stitch. Complete the row as usual **(fig. 33)**.

In the following row, work a herringbone stitch that connects to the first and third beads added for the decrease, skipping the middle increase bead **(fig. 34)**.

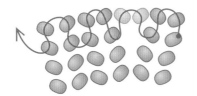

fig. 27

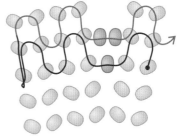

fig. 28

fig. 29

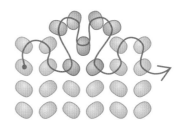

fig. 30

fig. 31

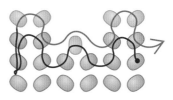

fig. 32

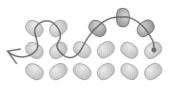

fig. 33

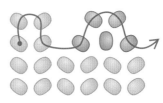

fig. 34

By simply using different-sized accent beads between columns of flat herringbone stitch, the spaces expand and contract to form a dynamic pattern. Stitch several panels together into a cuff, then finish with tubular herringbone toggle bars. • by *Melinda Barta*

reflections

TECHNIQUES
Flat and tubular herringbone stitch

Square stitch

Ladder stitch

Right-angle weave variation

MATERIALS
1 g dark steel/sage green permanent galvanized size 15° Japanese seed beads (A)

7 g dark steel/sage green permanent galvanized size 11° Japanese seed beads (B)

1 g metallic red copper size 11° Japanese seed beads (C)

62 antique copper size 8° seed beads (D)

38 brown iris 5mm pressed-glass melon rounds (E)

30 metallic amethyst 4mm pressed-glass rounds or druks (F)

30 brown iris 3mm fire-polished rounds (G)

1" (2.5 cm) of sterling silver 22-gauge wire

Smoke 6 lb braided beading thread

TOOLS
Scissors

Size 10 and 12 beading needles

Wire cutters

FINISHED SIZE
6⅝" (16.5 cm)

1 Panels. Use square stitch for the starting row and flat herringbone stitch for all following rows to form rectangular beaded components:

ROW 1: Use 6' (183 cm) of thread to string 2B; pass through the first 2 beads to form a square stitch. *String 7A and 2B; pass through the last 2B strung. String 3A and 2B; pass through the last 2B strung. Repeat from *. String 7A and 2B; pass through the last 2B strung twice. Knot the working thread twice around the thread loop between beads. Pass back through the last B strung (**fig. 1**). Pull on the tail thread and push the square stitches toward the last 2B strung to remove any slack in the strand. Orient the stitches and sets of A according to **fig. 1**, with the sets of A exiting downward from the B pairs.

ROW 2: String 2B; pass down through the next B of Row 1. String 1E; pass up through the following B of Row 1. String 2B; pass down through the next B of Row 1. String 1C; pass up through the following B of Row 1. Repeat from the beginning of this row again. String 2B; pass down through the next B of Row 1. String 1E; pass up through the following B of Row 1. String 2B; pass down through the next B of Row 1. Knot the tail and working threads and pass back through the first B of Row 1 and the final B of Row 2 (**fig. 2**).

ROW 3: String 4B, then pass down through the next 2B (B of Row 2 and B of Row 1), through the nearest accent bead (E or C) of Row 2, and up through the 2 following B (B of Row 1 and B of Row 2); repeat four times. String 4B; pass down through the next B of Row 2. *Note:* Step up for this and subsequent rows by looping the thread around the nearest connecting threads of the previous row and passing back up through the bead just exited and the last bead(s) added in the current row (**fig. 3**).

ROW 4: String 4B; pass down through the next top B of Row 3. String 1F; pass up through the following top B of Row 3. String 4B; pass down through the next 2B of Row 3. String 1D; pass up through the following 2B of Row 3. Repeat from the beginning of this row again. String 4B; pass down through the next top B of Row 3. String 1F; pass up through the following top B of Row 3. String 4B; pass down through the next top B of Row 3 (**fig. 4**).

ROW 5: String 4B; pass down through the next top B of Row 4. String 1G; pass up through the following top B of Row 4. String 4B; pass down through the next 2B of Row 4. String 1G; pass up through the following 2B of Row 4. Repeat from the beginning of this row again. String 4B; pass down through

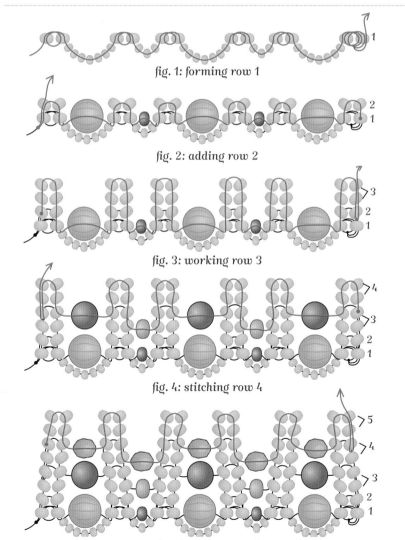

fig. 1: forming row 1

fig. 2: adding row 2

fig. 3: working row 3

fig. 4: stitching row 4

fig. 5: adding row 5

the next top B of Row 4. String 1G; pass up through the following top B of Row 4. String 4B; pass down through the next top B of Row 4 (**fig. 5**).

ROW 6: String 4B; pass down through the next top B of Row 5. String 1D; pass up through the following top B of Row 5. String 4B; pass down through the next 2B of Row 5. String 1F; pass up through the following 2B of Row 5. Repeat from the beginning of this row again. String 4B; pass down through the next top B of Row 5. String 1D; pass up through the following top B of Row 5. String 4B; pass down through the next top B of Row 5 (**fig. 6**).

ROW 7: String 4B; pass down through the next top B of Row 6. String 1C; pass up through the following top B of Row 6. String 4B; pass down through the next top B of Row 6. String 1E; pass up through the following top B of Row 6. Repeat from the beginning of this row again. String 4B; pass down through the next top B of Row 6. String 1C; pass up through the following top B of Row 6. String 4B; pass down through the next top B of Row 6 (**fig. 7**).

ROW 8: String 4B; pass down through the next top B of Row 7. String 1D; pass up through the following top B of Row 7. String 4B; pass down through the next 3B (2B of Row 7 and 1B of Row 6). Pass through the nearest E and up through the following 3B (top B of Row 6 and 2B of Row 7). Repeat from the beginning of this row again. String 4B; pass down through the next top B of Row 7. String 1D; pass up through the following top B of Row 7. String 4B; pass down through the next top B of Row 7 (**fig. 8, green**).

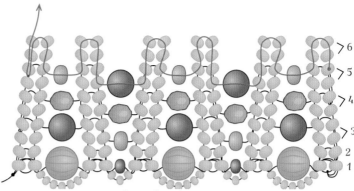

fig. 6: forming row 6

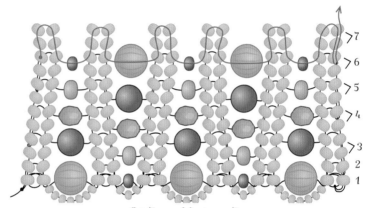

fig. 7: working row 7

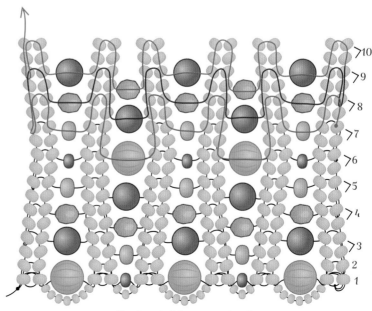

fig. 8: stitching rows 8–10

35

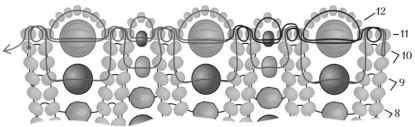

fig. 9: adding rows 11 and 12

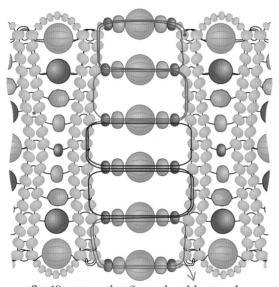

fig. 10: connecting 2 panels with strands

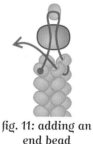

fig. 11: adding an end bead

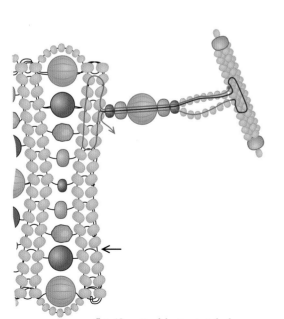

fig. 12: attaching a toggle bar

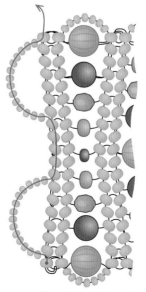

fig. 13: forming the clasp loops

ROW 9: String 4B; pass down through the next top B of Row 8. String 1G; pass up through the following top B of Row 8. String 4B; pass down through the next 2B of Row 8. String 1F; pass up through the following 2B of Row 8. Repeat from the beginning of this row again. String 4B; pass down through the next top B of Row 8. String 1G; pass up through the following top B of Row 8. String 4B; pass down through the next top B of Row 8 **(fig. 8, blue)**.

ROW 10: String 4B; pass down through the next top B of Row 9. String 1F; pass up through the following top B of Row 9. String 4B; pass down through the next 2B of Row 9. String 1G; pass up through the following 2B of Row 9. Repeat from the beginning of this row again. String 4B; pass down through the next top B of Row 9. String 1F; pass up through the following top B of Row 9. String 4B; pass down through the next top B of Row 9 **(fig. 8, red)**.

ROW 11: String 2B; pass down through the next 3B (2B of Row 10 and top B of Row 9). Pass through the nearest F and up through the following 3B (top B of Row 9 and 2B of Row 10). String 2B; pass down through the next 2B of Row 10. String 1D; pass up through the following 2B of Row 10. Repeat from the beginning of this row again. String 2B; pass down through the next 3B (2B of Row 10 and top B of Row 9). Pass through the nearest F and up through the following 3B (top B of Row 9 and 2B of Row 10). String 2B; pass down through the next top B of Row 10 **(fig. 9, green)**.

ROW 12: Square-stitch together the last 2B of Row 11. **String 1E; pass up through the next B of Row 11. String 7A; pass down through the last B exited before the E just added. Pass through the E and square-stitch together the next 2B of Row 11. String 1C; pass up through the nearest B of Row 11. String 3A; pass down through the last B exited before the C just added. Pass through the C and square-stitch together the next 2B of Row 11 **(fig. 9, blue)**. Repeat from **. String 1E; pass up through the following B of Row 11. String 7A; pass down through the last B exited before the E just added. Pass through the E and square-stitch together the last 2B of Row 11 **(fig. 9, red)**. Secure and trim the tail thread. Weave the working thread through beads to exit away from the beadwork, up through the last bead exited. Repeat this entire step twice for a total of 3 panels.

2 Joins. Use a variation of right-angle weave to join the panels with short bead strands:

UNIT 1: Using the working thread of 1 panel, string 1A, 1C, 1D, 1E, 1D, 1C, and 1A; pass down through the top-right 3B of a second panel, positioning the panels side by side. String 1C, 1D, 1E, 1D, and 1C; pass up through the top 3B of the right panel. Weave through beads to exit the C/D/E/D/C just added **(fig. 10, purple)**.

UNIT 2: Skip 1B of the nearest panel and pass down through the next 3B. String 1C, 1D, 1E, 1D, and 1C; pass up through the first 3B of the next 4B on the opposite panel. Weave through beads to exit the C/D/E/D/C just added **(fig. 10, green)**.

UNITS 3 AND 4: Repeat Unit 2 twice **(fig. 10, blue)**.

UNIT 5: Repeat Unit 2, this time stringing 1A, 1C, 1D, 1E, 1D, 1C, and 1A to mirror the top strand of Unit 1 **(fig. 10, red)**. Secure the thread and trim.

Using the working thread of the remaining panel, repeat this entire step to connect the remaining panel to the end of one just joined.

3 Toggle bars. Use tubular herringbone stitch to form toggle bars:

TUBE ROUND 1: Use 4' (122 cm) of new thread to ladder-stitch 4A, leaving a 12" (30.5 cm) tail. Ladder-stitch the first and last A to form a ring.

TUBE ROUNDS 2–13: String 2A, then pass down through the next A of the previous round and up through the following A of the previous round; repeat. Step up for the next and subsequent

rounds by passing through the first bead of the current round. Continue in tubular herringbone stitch for a total of 13 rounds. Stitch through the last round of beads following a ladder-stitch thread path. Exit away from the beadwork from one end A.

WIRE: Insert ½" (1.3 cm) of wire inside the tube and hold in place while finishing the ends.

ENDS: String 1D and 1A; pass back through the D and the A of Round 13 opposite the last one exited and up through the following A of Round 13 **(fig. 11)**. Repeat the thread path to center the D over the end of the tube and connect to all end A of Round 13. Weave through beads to exit 6A from the end of the tube, toward the center. Use the tail thread to finish the opposite end of the tube in the same manner. Secure the tail thread and trim.

ATTACH: String 7A, 1C, 1D, 1E, 1D, and 1C; pass up through the fourth B from the top right end bead at one end of the bracelet. Weave through beads to exit toward the B last entered **(fig. 12, green).** *Note:* This places the connection between the fourth and fifth B of the bracelet end. Weave through the beads just added and through beads of the tube to exit the sixth A from the other end of the tube **(fig. 12, blue).** String 7A; pass through the C/D/E/D/C and the nearest B at the end of the bracelet **(fig. 12, red).** Repeat the thread path several times to reinforce. Secure the thread and trim. Repeat this entire step for a second toggle bar. Attach it between the fifteenth and sixteenth B (indicated with black arrow in **fig. 12**) at the same end of the bracelet.

4 **Clasp loops.** Start 12" (30.5 cm) of new thread that exits toward the beadwork from one end B of the bracelet. String 14A; skip 6 end B and pass through the next 5 end B. String 14A; pass through the final end B **(fig. 13).** Check that the toggle bars can pass easily through the loops while ensuring that the loops aren't so loose that the toggles can slip out. If needed, remove the needle and the beads just placed, then adjust the number of A in the loops. Weave through beads to reinforce the thread path. Secure the thread and trim.

TIP

- When working 4 beads in a single herringbone stitch, make sure you pull tight to snap them into place.

DESIGN OPTION

Timeless Cuff

BY MELINDA BARTA

In lieu of stitching short panels, work the entire length of the bracelet at once as shown in this gold sample with peach and pink accent beads, stitched by Katie Nelson. Add short ribbons to the ends for an alternate closure or add long ribbons to wear this as a sweet headband or bold choker.

MATERIALS

0.5 g 24k gold electroplate size 15° Japanese seed beads

0.5 g matte metallic 24k gold electroplate size 15° Japanese seed beads

4 g gold Duracoat galvanized size 11° Japanese seed beads

4 g matte metallic 24k gold size 11° Japanese seed beads

1 g mauve-lined gold size 11° Japanese seed beads

46 rose-lined clear size 11° sharp triangles

35 opaque rose/gold topaz luster 5mm pressed-glass melon rounds

46 opaque rose/gold topaz luster 4mm pressed-glass rounds or druks

46 milky rose/bronze Vega 3mm fire-polished rounds

1 gold-plated 19×28mm 5-strand decorative box clasp

Tan One-G nylon beading thread

TOOLS

Scissors

Size 10 and 12 beading needles

FINISHED SIZE

7½" (19 cm)

1 BAND. Repeat Step 1 for the Reflections cuff (page 34), alternating 24k gold electroplate size 15°s and matte metallic 24k gold electroplate size 15°s for A. For B, alternate gold Duracoat galvanized size 11°s and matte metallic 24k gold size 11°s. Use mauve-lined gold size 11°s for C, triangles for D, opaque rose/gold topaz luster melon rounds for E, opaque rose/gold topaz luster 4mm rounds for F, and milky rose/bronze Vega 3mm rounds for G. *Note:* The two finishes (shiny and matte) of gold beads used for A and B are alternated so the diamond shapes are framed by the shiny gold beads (see photo for placement). To make a 6⅞" (17.2 cm) wide band, form

Row 1 with 24 pairs of ladder-stitch beads (and the alternating 3- and 7-bead nets in between as in Row 1 for the Reflections cuff). Increase the repeats in the following rounds accordingly. When working Row 2, be sure to hold the beadwork so the strand of Row 1 beads doesn't twist. This twisting isn't problematic when working the narrow panels in the Reflections cuff, but twisting is more common when working wide bands.

2 CLASP. Use 18" (45.5 cm) of new thread to sew one half of the clasp to one end of the band so the clasp loops are concealed by the end column. Secure the thread and trim. Repeat this entire step using the other half of the clasp.

Ribbonlike sections of silvery flat herringbone-stitched triangles create a subtle chevron pattern interspersed with lines of shimmering crystal bicones. With four triangles in each stitch, the rows work up quickly, so you can make this tonight and wear it tomorrow. ● *by Carole Ohl*

chiffon ribbon cuff

TECHNIQUES
Ladder stitch

Flat herringbone stitch

MATERIALS
14 g metallic bronze–lined clear size 11° Japanese sharp triangles (A)

49 crystal comet argent light 3mm crystal bicones (B)

1 sterling silver 15×27mm 5-strand rectangle box clasp with inset cubic zirconias

Smoke 6 lb braided beading thread

TOOLS
Scissors

Size 10 or 12 beading needles

FINISHED SIZE
6½" (16.5 cm)

NOTE
The instructions given are for the silver colorway. For information on the gold variation, see page 43.

1 Band. Work rows of flat herringbone stitch, with in-column crystal bicone accents, off of a ladder-stitched base row:

ROW 1: Add a needle to the center of 10' (305 cm) of thread and bring the ends together to form a 5' (152.5 cm) doubled thread. Ladder-stitch a strip 2A high and 14A wide, leaving an 18" (45.5 cm) tail. Orient the strip so you're exiting the right end of the beadwork, up through the last bead added **(fig. 1)**.

ROW 2: String 4A, pass down through the next 2 ladder-stitched A, then pass up through the 2 following ladder-stitched A; repeat six times across to add a total of 28A. Loop around threads under Row 1; pass back up through the 2 end A and the last 2A added **(fig. 2)**.

ROW 3: Work 7 herringbone stitches with 4A in each stitch to add a total of 28A. *Note:* Step up for this and subsequent rows by looping the thread around the nearest connecting threads of the previous rows and passing back up through the bead just exited and the last 2A added in the current row **(fig. 3, green)**.

ROW 4: String 1B and 4A, then pass back through the B, down through the next A of the previous row, and up through the following A of the previous row **(fig. 3, blue)**; repeat six times to add a total of 7B and 28A **(fig. 3, red)**.

ROWS 5–7: Repeat Row 3 three times.

ROW 8: Repeat Row 4.

ROWS 9–28: Repeat Rows 5–8 five times.

ROWS 29 AND 30: Repeat Row 3 twice. Stitch back through the beads of Row 30 following a ladder-stitch thread path to tighten the beads.

fig. 1: ladder-stitching row 1

fig. 2: herringbone-stitching row 2

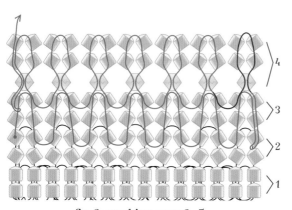

fig. 3: working rows 3–5

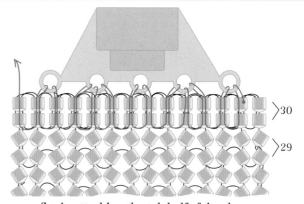

fig. 4: attaching the tab half of the clasp

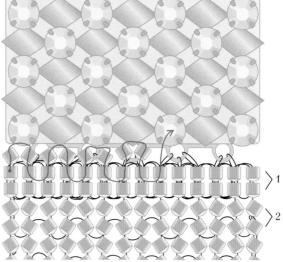

fig. 5: working the clasp cover row [starting stitches of row shown for clarity]

2 Finishing. Attach the clasp to the ends of the band:

TAB HALF: Weave through beads to exit away from the beadwork 1A in from one end of Row 30. Pass through the first loop of the tab half of the clasp, back through the A last exited and the A below it, and up through the next 2A of Row 30; repeat across the row to secure all clasp loops to the end of the band, passing through the nearest clasp loop (**fig. 4**). Secure the thread and trim.

BOX HALF ATTACHMENT: Weave the tail thread through beads to exit away from the beadwork from an end A of Row 1. Attach the loops of the box half of the clasp using the same technique as for the tab half of the clasp, centering the clasp at the end of the band. Do not trim the thread; exit away from the beadwork from an end A of Row 1.

BOX HALF COVER: To conceal the clasp loops, work a row of herringbone stitch with 2A in each stitch (**fig. 5**). Stitch back through the beads of this row following a ladder-stitch thread path to tighten the beads. Secure the thread and trim.

TIPS

- To make it easier to work near the clasp on the final row, fold the clasp down so the clasp connectors are more available.

- Use only the best, most consistent triangles. If one happens to break, you may have to tear out a row or two to replace the broken bead; otherwise, threads will show.

- When making a cuff, Carole chooses her clasp first because trying to find a large clasp after a cuff is completed can be difficult. Once she chooses the clasp that matches her idea, then it's easier to choose bead colors to work with the clasp. In this case, she wanted the silver accents to match the color of the clasp. Plus, by choosing the clasp first, she knew exactly how wide to make the cuff.

- Sometimes when Carole is unsure of which color combination to use, she works up a section or component in a different color. Many of these "samplers" become favorite bracelets that can be worn with anything. For this project, you can alternate the rows of herringbone for a striped effect, using the same bicones to tie the colors all together.

- You can make each section shorter or longer, depending on how many crystals you have available. If you prefer lots of bling, make additional shorter sections.

DESIGN OPTION

BY CAROLE OHL
Use metallic green iris size 11° Japanese sharp triangles and gold size 8° seed beads to form this shimmering variation.

By starting Row 1 with 20 triangles, the ends of the finished cuff measure 1½" (3.8 cm) wide, perfect for the 17×37mm rectangular box clasp.

DESIGN OPTION

Filigree Square Bracelet

BY MELINDA BARTA

Inspired by the way Carole broke up sections of flat herringbone with embellishment beads, I created a spin on her pattern using bugle, cube, and copper seed beads. Filigree adds a romantic touch in the central brass square and in the decorative bead caps used for the clasp.

MATERIALS

1 g bronze 1.8mm cubes

3 g burgundy iris 3mm (size 1) bugle beads

1 g antique copper size 8° seed beads

1 g matte burgundy size 11° Japanese seed beads

2 brass 13mm filigree bead caps

1 brass 30mm filigree square

Smoke 4 lb and 6 lb braided beading thread

TOOLS

Scissors

Size 12 beading needle

FINISHED SIZE

7¼" (18.5 cm)

1 HERRINGBONE STRIPS.

Using the techniques covered in Carole's Chiffon Ribbon Cuff (page 40), form 2 strips of beadwork to frame the filigree square:

ROW 1: Add a needle to the center of 9' (274 cm) of 4 lb thread and bring the ends together to form a doubled thread. Ladder-stitch a strip 16 cubes long. *Note:* Unless otherwise indicated, continue to work the entire project with doubled 4 lb thread.

ROWS 2–4: Work 3 rows of flat herringbone stitch with 2 bugles in each stitch. *Note:* Continue to work 2 bugles in each stitch, not 4 beads in each stitch as in the Chiffon Ribbon Cuff.

ROW 5: Add 1 cube below each herringbone pair of bugles, using the same technique as adding bicones in Step 1, Row 4 of the Chiffon Ribbon Cuff.

ROWS 6 AND 7: Work flat herringbone stitch with 2 bugles in each stitch.

ROW 8: Add 1 cube/1 size 8°/1 cube below each herringbone pair of bugles, using the same technique as adding bicones in Step 1, Row 4 of the Chiffon Ribbon Cuff.

ROWS 9–14: Repeat Rows 3–8 of this project.

ROWS 15 AND 16: Work 2 rows of flat herringbone stitch with 2 bugles in each stitch.

ROW 17 (CONNECTION): Exiting up through an end bugle, *string 1 size 8° and pass through an opening at one corner of the filigree square. Pass back through the size 8°, the next bugle of Row 16, and up through the following bugle of Row 16. Repeat from * across Row 16, evenly spacing the beadwork along the filigree square. If desired, weave back through the beads of this row and Row 16, adding 1 horizontal bugle between each size 8° to cover the threads that connect to the filigree; the holes of these bugles will sit perpendicular to the holes of the size 8°s. Secure the thread and trim.

Repeat this entire step for a second herringbone strip that connects to the other side of the filigree square. If desired, gently bend the filigree square to match the curve of your wrist.

2 FINISHING. Attach bead caps and form clasp loops:

CAPS: Start 2' (61 cm) of 6 lb thread that exits toward the beadwork from the fourth cube from one end of Row 1. String 4 size 11°s, 1 cap (wide end first), and 1 size 11°; pass back through the cap, the 4 size 11°s, and the next cube of Row 1 to form a fringe. Repeat the thread path twice to reinforce. Weave through beads to exit the fourth bead from the other end of Row 1 and form a second fringe as before. Secure the thread and trim.

CLASP LOOPS: Start 2' (61 cm) of 6 lb thread that exits away from the beadwork from the fourth cube from one end of Row 1, on the end of the bracelet opposite the caps. String 1 size 11°, 1 cube, and 26 size 11°s; pass back through the cube, the first size 11° added, and the next cube of Row 1 to form a loop. If needed, adjust the number of beads in the loop to accommodate the caps. Repeat the thread path twice to reinforce. Weave through beads to exit the fourth bead from the other end of Row 1 and form a second loop as before. Secure the thread and trim.

Use herringbone-stitch increases to form the flared ends of this art deco–inspired necklace. A bezeled crystal oval makes a focal point that's as beautiful as the French actress for whom the piece is named.
● by Jean Campbell

jeanne moreau

TECHNIQUES
Ladder stitch

Flat and tubular herringbone stitch

Square stitch

Fringe

Picot

Right-angle weave

Tubular peyote stitch

MATERIALS
1 g metallic silver size 15° seed beads (A)

3 g metallic denim size 11° seed beads (B)

1 g metallic silver size 11° seed beads (C)

15 g metallic silver size 8° seed beads (D)

6 Montana blue 3mm crystal rounds (E)

8 Tahitian-look 6mm crystal pearl rounds (F)

1 Tahitian-look 12mm crystal pearl round

1 Montana 22×30mm crystal faceted oval fancy stone

Crystal 6 lb braided beading thread

TOOLS
Scissors

Size 12 sharp beading needle

FINISHED SIZE
17" (43 cm)

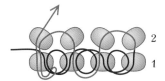

fig. 1: forming rows 1 and
2 of the strap flare

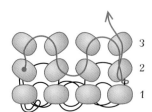

fig. 2: adding row 3 of
the strap flare

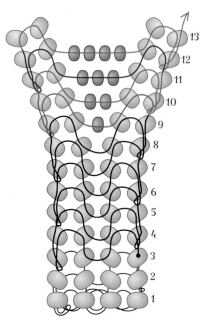

fig. 3: working rows 4–13 of
the strap flare

1 Strap flare. Form the flared end of one side of the necklace using flat herringbone stitch:

FLARE ROW 1: Use 6' (183 cm) of thread to form a loose strip of ladder stitch 4D long. Orient the strip so you're exiting the right end of the beadwork, up through the last bead added (**fig. 1, blue**).

FLARE ROW 2: String 2D; pass down through the next D of Flare Row 1 and up through the following D. String 2D; pass down through the next D of Flare Row 1. Loop around threads under Flare Row 1; pass back up through the end D of Flare Row 1 and the last D added in Flare Row 2 (**fig. 1, red**).

FLARE ROW 3: String 2D; pass down through the next D of the previous row and up through the following D. String 2D; pass down through the next D of the previous row (**fig. 2**). *Note:* Step up for this and subsequent rows by looping the thread around the nearest connecting threads of the previous rows, and passing back up through the bead just exited and the last bead added in the current row.

FLARE ROWS 4–9: Repeat Flare Row 3 six times (**fig. 3, black**).

FLARE ROW 10: String 2D; pass down through the next D of Flare Row 9 (a herringbone stitch). String 1B (an increase bead); pass up through the following D of Flare Row 9. String 2D; pass down through the next D of Flare Row 9 (a herringbone stitch) and step up (**fig. 3, purple**).

Repeat Flare Row 10 in Flare Rows 11–19, adding one 2D herringbone stitch, increase beads, and one 2D herringbone stitch. Use the beads (or sequence of beads) listed for each row below for the increase that occurs between the herringbone columns:

FLARE ROW 11: 2B (**fig. 3, green**).

FLARE ROW 12: 3B (**fig. 3, blue**).

FLARE ROW 13: 4B (**fig. 3, red**).

FLARE ROW 14: 2B, 1E, and 2B (**fig. 4, orange**).

FLARE ROW 15: 8B (**fig. 4, pink**).

FLARE ROW 16: 2B, 1E, 2B, 1E, and 2B (**fig. 4, purple**).

FLARE ROW 17: 4B, 1F, and 4B (**fig. 4, green**).

FLARE ROW 18: 2B, 1F, 2B, 1F, and 2B (**fig. 4, blue**).

FLARE ROW 19: 7B, 1F, and 7B (**fig. 4, red**).

FLARE ROW 20: String 1D; pass through the next D of Flare Row 19. String 15D (increase beads); pass up through the following D of Flare Row 19. String 1D; pass down through the next D of Flare Row 19 and step up. Pass back through the last D added (**fig. 5, green**).

FLARE ROW 21: String 2D; pass through the last D added in the Flare Row 20 increase and through the second D just added. *String 1D; pass through the next D of the Flare Row 20 increase and the D just added. Repeat square-stitching from * thirteen times to add a total of 16D across the row. String 1D and pass through the first D added in Flare Row 20. Weave through beads to exit from the center D of this row (**fig. 5, blue**).

PICOT: String 3D; pass through the last D exited on Flare Row 21 to form a picot. Repeat the thread path twice to reinforce. Weave through beads to exit between the twelfth and thirteenth increase D of Flare Row 20 (**fig. 5, red**).

2 **Flare top.** Secure the rows of the flare by connecting them with a variation of right-angle weave and embellish the top:

SECURE ROW 1: String 1B; pass back through the fourth through seventh B and F of Flare Row 19. String 1B; pass through the seventh to ninth increase D of Flare Row 20. String 1B; pass through the F and eighth through eleventh D of Flare Row 19. String 1B; pass through the fourth to ninth increase D of Flare Row 20. Weave through beads to exit from the eleventh B of Flare Row 19 (**fig. 6, purple**).

SECURE ROW 2: String 1B; pass through the nearest F/2B/F of Flare Row 18. String 1B; pass through the fourth through seventh B, the F, and the eighth through eleventh B of Flare Row 19. Pass through the first B added in this row and the nearest F/2B/F of Flare Row 18 (**fig. 6, green**).

SECURE ROW 3: String 1B; pass through the second through fourth B, the F, and the next 3B of Flare Row 17. String 1B; pass through the nearest F/2B/F of Flare Row 18. Weave through beads to exit the F of Flare Row 17 (**Fig. 6, blue**).

SECURE ROW 4: String 1B; pass through the center E/2B/E of Flare Row 16. String 1B; pass

through the F of Flare Row 17 (**fig. 6, red**).

Repeat the thread path for the secure rows, exiting the center F of Flare Row 17 when done.

EMBELLISHMENT: String 3B, 1D, and 3B; pass through the F of Flare Row 19 so the strand sits diagonally between the 2F of Flare Row 18. String 3B; pass back through the last D added. String 3B; pass through the F of Flare Row 17 (**fig. 7, green**). Repeat the thread path to reinforce. Weave through beads to exit from 1F of Flare Row 18, toward the center of the flare (**fig. 7, blue**). Pass the working thread over the threads that

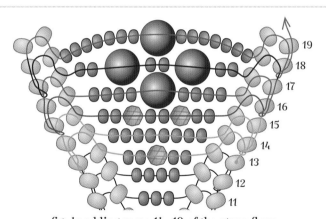

fig. 4: adding rows 14–19 of the strap flare

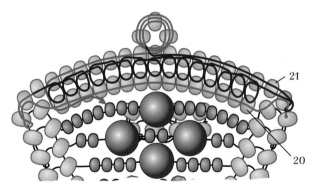

fig. 5: forming rows 20 and 21 and the picot

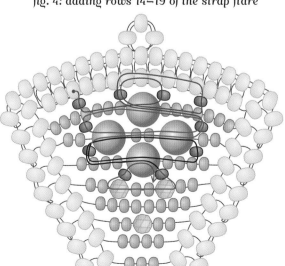

fig. 6: working secure rows 1–4 of the flare top

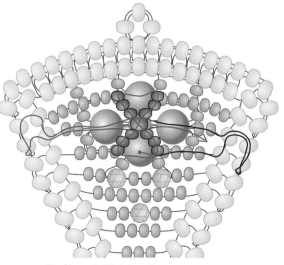

fig. 7: embellishing the secure rows

fig. 8: starting the strap rope

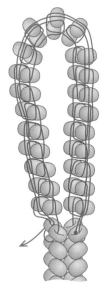

fig. 9: square-stitching the clasp loop

fig. 10: adding the clasp toggle

added the D in this embellishment, just above the D; pass through the next F of Flare Row 18. Weave through beads to pass back through the last F exited. Pass the working thread over the threads that added the D in this embellishment, just below the D; pass through the next F of Flare Row 18 (**fig. 7, red**). Repeat the thread path to reinforce. *Note:* This pulls the cross of pearls down against the increase beads of Flare Rows 17–19. Secure the threads and trim.

3 Strap rope. Use tubular herringbone stitch to form the rope section of the strap:

STARTING ROUND: Rotate the work 180°. Start 6' (183 cm) of new thread that exits from an end D at the bottom of Flare Row 1. Pinch the row together so the outer edges fold down in the same direction as the outer edges of the flare. Square-stitch the first and last D to form a ring (**fig. 8, green**).

FOLLOWING ROUNDS: String 2D, then pass down through the next D of the previous round and up through the next D of the previous round (**fig. 8, blue**); repeat. Step up for the next and subsequent rounds by passing through the first bead of the current round (**fig. 8, red**). Continue working rounds in the same manner until the rope measures 6" (15 cm) or the desired length. Don't trim the thread; set aside.

Repeat Steps 1–3 for a second strap.

4. Clasp ring. Use the working thread at the end of one strap to square-stitch a strip 2D across and 21 rows long. Fold the strip so the final beads meet the other side of the rope and, making sure the strip isn't twisted, square-stitch the beads together to form a ring (**fig. 9**). Secure the thread and trim. Set aside.

5. Clasp toggle. Use the working thread at the end of the remaining strap to string 1D; pass down through the D on the other side of the rope that's diagonal to the one just exited and up through the next D. Pass through the D just added and pass down through the D on the other side of the rope that's diagonal to the one just exited and up through the next D. Pass through the D just added (**fig. 10, blue**). String 1D, the 12mm pearl, and 3C; pass back through the pearl and the D below to form a fringe with a picot on top.

Pass through the first D added in this step (**fig. 10, red**). Repeat the entire thread path several times to reinforce. Secure the thread and trim. Set aside.

6. Rings. Square-stitch thin strips and join them into rings that cover the straps:

ROW 1: Use 3' (91.5 cm) of thread to string 14D, leaving a 6" (15 cm) tail.

ROW 2: String 1D; pass through the last D of the previous row, forming the first square stitch. String 1D; pass through the second-to-last D of the previous row, forming the second square stitch. Continue square-stitching down Row 1 with 1D in each stitch (**fig. 11**). Slide the ring onto one strap so that it covers the starting round of the rope. Neatly stitch the ring to the strap so it doesn't slide; secure the thread and trim.

Repeat this entire step to form a ring that covers the starting round of the other strap's rope.

7. Bezel. Use right-angle weave and tubular peyote stitch to bead a bezel for the crystal oval:

BEZEL ROUND 1, UNIT 1: Use 6' (183 cm) of thread to string 4D; pass through the first 3D strung (**fig. 12, blue**).

BEZEL ROUND 1, UNITS 2–20: String 3D, then pass through the last D exited in the previous unit and the first 2D just strung (**fig. 12, red**); repeat eighteen times for a total of 20 units.

BEZEL ROUND 1, UNIT 21: Fold the strip in half, making sure it isn't twisted. String 1D; pass back through the end bead of Unit 1. String 1D; pass through the end bead of Unit 20 to form a ring. Exit from the top D (**fig. 13**).

TIPS

• Cull your size 8° beads. Because they are a bit larger, their irregularities are more noticeable, especially on the flare and strap.

• Spend time reinforcing the Flare Rows, Secure Rows, and Embellishment at the center of each flare—this will ensure that they keep their shape.

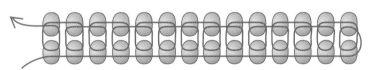

fig. 11: forming rows 1 and 2 of a ring

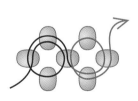

fig. 12: working units 1 and 2 of bezel round 1

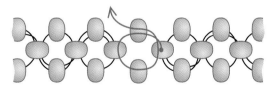

fig. 13: stitching the right-angle-weave strip into a ring

DESIGN OPTION

BY JEAN CAMPBELL

By repeating the flare pattern for the Jeanne Moreau necklace several times and layering the flares, you can create a gorgeous coordinating bracelet.

Start by forming 3 large flares, then complete 2 strips that include smaller, layered clasp flares:

LARGE FLARES: Repeat Steps 1 and 2 of the necklace (pages 48–50) to form 3 large flares.

STRIP 1: Off the bottom of 1 large flare (the leftmost flare of the focal shown in the photo), work a 4" (10 cm) stem of flat herringbone stitch, then form a smaller (fourth) clasp flare off the other end (this will form the inside layer of the flare near the clasp).

STRIP 2: Off the bottom of a second large flare (the rightmost flare of the focal shown in the photo), form the second strip by working ¾" (2 cm) of flat herringbone stitch, a few rows with seed bead and crystal increases and decreases, another ¾" (2 cm) of flat herringbone stitch, and a few more rows of increases and decreases. Finally, form a smaller (fifth) flare that matches the clasp flare of Strip 1, but incorporates the central pearl of the matching small clasp flare on Strip 1 so that the small flares become connected. *Note:* Layer this strip on top of Strip 1 when working the small clasp flare; Strip 2 forms the outside of the bracelet.

ASSEMBLY: Use square stitch to connect the edges the small clasp flares so they look like 1 thick flare, then continue connecting the edges of Strips 1 and 2. Tuck the remaining large flare between the 2 large flares and stitch it to the others in the same manner. Use D to form a tab of right-angle weave off the end of the small clasp flares; sew a snap to the tab. Stitch the other side of the snap to the inside tip of the focal's leftmost large flare.

BEZEL ROUND 2: String 1C and pass through the next top D of Round 1; repeat twenty times to peyote-stitch a total of 21C. Step up for the next and subsequent rounds by passing through the first bead added in the current round **(fig. 14, purple)**.

BEZEL ROUNDS 3 AND 4: Work tubular peyote stitch with 1C in each stitch for a total of 2 rounds **(fig. 14, green)**.

BEZEL ROUND 5: Work tubular peyote stitch with 1A in each stitch. Weave through beads to exit from the other side of Round 1 **(fig. 14, blue)**.

BEZEL ROUNDS 6–8: Place the crystal oval in the beadwork so the face touches Bezel Rounds 4 and 5. Repeat Bezel Rounds 2 and 3, then repeat Bezel Round 5 to bezel the back of the oval **(fig. 14, red)**. Weave through beads to exit from a top D of Bezel Round 1, on the front of the bezel, just right of the top center of the oval.

CONNECT: String the middle D of the picot at the end of one strap's flare, taking care that both the flare and the bezel face up. Pass through the next top D of Bezel Round 1; weave through beads to pass back through the middle D of the picot **(fig. 15, blue)**. Weave through beads of the picot and bezel to pass back through the first D of Bezel Round 1 exited in this section **(fig. 15, red)**. Repeat the thread path several times to reinforce. Secure the thread and trim. Repeat to connect the second strap to the other side of the bezel.

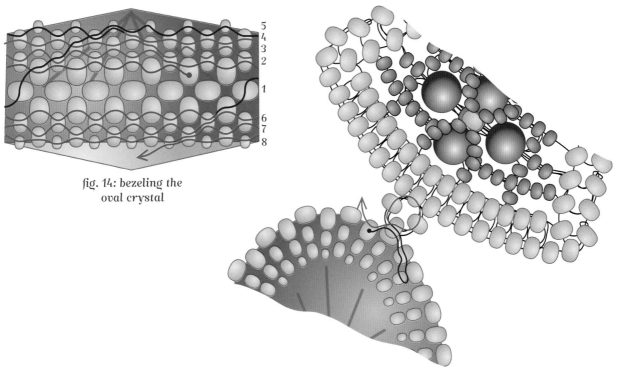

fig. 14: bezeling the
oval crystal

fig. 15: connecting the bezel and flare

circular herringbone stitch

Circular herringbone stitch begins with a ring of beads (simply strung or often peyote-stitched) and grows outward from one round to the next. When you desire a flat piece of beadwork, add increase beads between columns, offsetting the distinct look of angled herringbone beads. Methodical and repetitive, circular herringbone is fun to stitch, and its versatility abounds.

Use a quick-to-stitch combination of circular peyote and herringbone stitches to form sweet single- and double-layer flowers in my **Graceful Garland** necklace. Join the petals end-to-end for the look of a beautiful garland and create a clean finish with a hidden snap clasp between two of the floral components. Also see my variation on the design, **Rose Garden Necklace.**

In her **Starbright Bracelet,** Kelly Wiese shows off the versatility of circular herringbone stitch with her clever technique for bezeling crystal chatons. Connect the components with sparkling nets of crystals and seed beads to form an elegant, sophisticated bracelet.

Start with two simple circular herringbone flowers, then zip up the outside edges to form beautifully weighted charms. Use them to adorn strands of gold and silver chain as I did in my **Gilded Blossoms** necklace or incorporate them into your own unique design. Also see my variation on the design, **Chocolate Flower Earrings.**

TECHNIQUES

counting

Because circular herringbone components are worked from the inside out, the innermost round is Round 1. Accent beads and other increase beads between columns can be challenging to count, so be sure to follow along the beads of a column when counting (**fig. 1**). Here, the blue beads in Rounds 3–4 are column beads, and the pink beads are between-column accent beads.

It's common for the first few rounds of circular herringbone to start with circular peyote stitch, so remember that the first ring of beads strung for circular peyote often make up both Rounds 1 *and* 2 (**fig. 2, blue**). Here, a third round of circular peyote stitch (**fig. 2, red**) is worked before beginning herringbone.

circular herringbone stitch

There are endless combinations of bead sizes and types used in this variation of herringbone. To keep circular herringbone pieces flat, you'll need to add beads between herringbone columns. Some designs

even incorporate sections of peyote stitch between columns. Learn the technique by following this sample, then play around with your own variations:

ROUND 1: String 6 size 11° seed beads. Pass through all of the beads again, tie a knot with the tail and working threads, and pass through the first bead strung (**fig. 3, green**).

ROUND 2: String 1 size 11° and pass through the next bead of Round 1; repeat five times to complete the round of circular peyote stitch. Step up through the first bead added in this round (**fig. 3, blue**).

ROUND 3: String 2 size 11°s and pass through the next bead of Round 1; repeat five times. Step up through the first bead added in this round (**fig. 3, red**). *Note:* This round is considered two-drop peyote stitch and adds the bead pairs that become the base of the following round's herringbone pairs.

ROUND 4: String 2 size 11°s and pass through the nearest bead of Round 3, then string 1 size 11° and pass up through the next bead of Round 3; repeat five times to add a total of 6 herringbone stitches with 1 size 11° between each column (**fig. 4**). *Note:* If the beadwork doesn't lie flat, consider using size 15°s in place of the 11°s between columns.

Continue working herringbone stitches at the top of each column and treat the beads between the columns with one of the following techniques. Don't be afraid to play around with alternate starts for Rounds 1 and 2, including the ones on page 57 and those featured in the following projects.

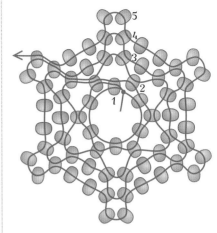

fig. 1

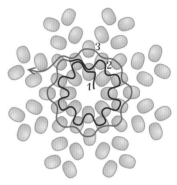

fig. 2

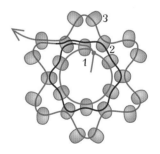

fig. 3

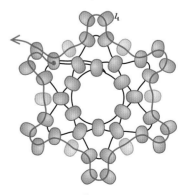

fig. 4

55

STRANDS BETWEEN COLUMNS

Repeat Round 4 as many times as desired, adding larger beads or more beads between columns to keep the work flat (**fig. 5**). This results in a flexible piece of beadwork that's a bit airy between the strands. If desired, you can go back and join the beads of these strands with square or other stitches, as Jean Campbell cleverly did in the flared sections of her Jeanne Moreau necklace (page 46).

PEYOTE BETWEEN COLUMNS

For a fuller, more solid structure between columns, work circular peyote stitch with 1 bead in each stitch. Notice how the bead count in each section of peyote stitch increases by 1 bead from one round to the next; this helps keep the beadwork flat (**fig. 6**). In this example, 15°s are worked between columns of 11°s to keep the work flat. You can also help keep the work flat by manipulating the beadwork in your hand after each round worked and by controlling your thread tension. (Too-tight tension can make the work cup.) See how-to information for peyote stitch on page 159.

ADDING MORE COLUMNS

Instead of just filling the space between columns with strands of beads or sections of circular peyote, it's possible to add more columns of herringbone stitch. To begin, work 1 round where the center of each peyote section has a stitch made with 2 beads (**fig. 7**). Use the thinnest beads in your bead stash for the pairs to keep the increase gradual. In the following round, begin stitching new herringbone columns off the pairs just added. Experiment with different bead-size combinations to make the work as flat or wavy as you desire.

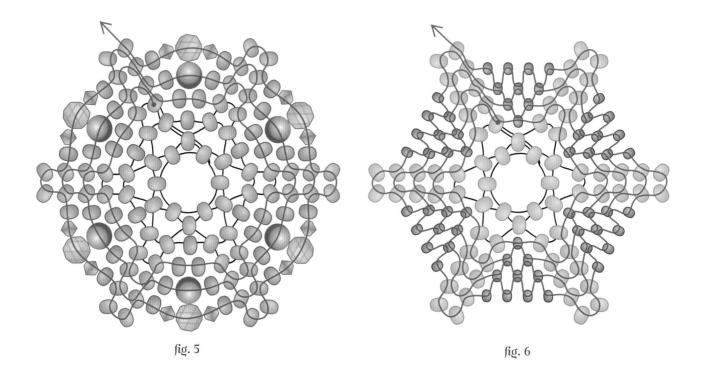

fig. 5

fig. 6

alternate starts

Although starting with a ring of beads or a few rounds of circular peyote stitch are the most common ways to begin circular herringbone, here are a few useful alternatives.

LADDER STITCH

When starting with a ring of ladder-stitched beads, use very relaxed tension so that the beads can roll outward, with the holes pointing away from the center. The beads will touch on the inside of the ring, but need to have spaces between their outside edges in order to lie flat (**fig. 8**).

BRICK STITCH

When beading around a center focal bead, work the first round with brick stitch to properly orient the beads for the following herringbone rounds. Start by stringing the focal bead and passing through it again (**fig. 9, blue**). Pass through the focal bead a third time to add a second foundation thread around the outside edge (**fig. 9, red**). If desired, repeat the thread paths to double up the foundation threads for added security.

Work brick stitches around the bead: String 2 beads and slide them down to the focal bead. Pass the needle under the foundation thread(s) and pass back up through the last bead added. Pull the thread snug to position the beads side by side (**fig. 10, blue**). *String 1 bead, pass the needle under the foundation threads, and pass back up through the last bead added. Pull the thread snug to position the new bead next to the previous one. Repeat from * to continue the round. Close the round by stitching through the first bead added using a brick-stitch thread path (**fig. 10, red**). Make sure the total number of beads in the round is an even number. Begin circular herringbone stitch as usual.

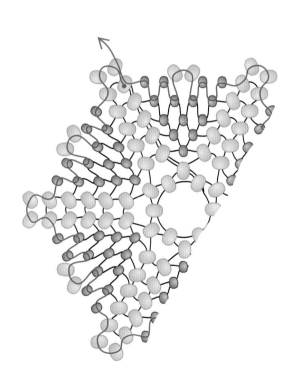

fig. 7

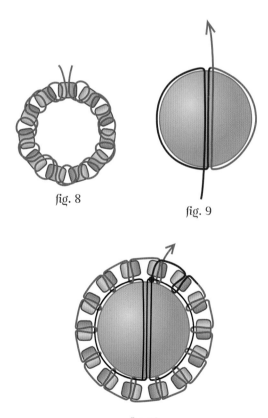

fig. 8

fig. 9

fig. 10

Cool shades of silver and purplish blue dress up this trail of flowers while the alternating two-layer flowers add lifelike dimension. A hidden clasp seamlessly continues the look of a garland. ● *by Melinda Barta*

graceful garland

TECHNIQUES

Circular herringbone stitch

Circular peyote stitch

Picot

Square stitch

MATERIALS

2 g nickel silver electroplate size 15° Japanese seed beads (A)

10 g gilt-lined silver/gray opal size 11° Japanese seed beads (B)

8 g metallic plum hematite size 11° Japanese seed beads (C)

115 hematite 3mm pressed-glass rounds (D)

1 silver size 1 (⅜" [1 cm]) snap set

2 gray ½" (1.3 cm) Ultrasuede squares

Smoke 6 lb braided beading thread

TOOLS

Scissors

Size 10 and 12 beading needles

Ballpoint pen

FINISHED SIZE

19½" (49.5 cm)

NOTE

Start with the size 10 needle and switch to the size 12 if you ever have trouble fitting the needle through beads.

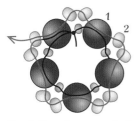

fig. 1: forming rounds 1 and 2

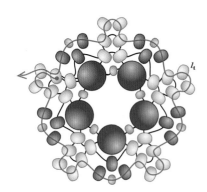

fig. 2: adding round 3

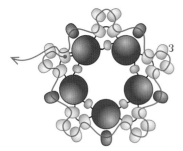

fig. 3: working round 4

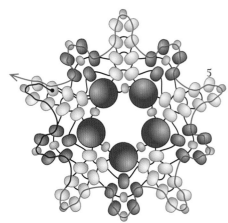

fig. 4: stitching round 5

1 Single-layer flowers.

Use circular herringbone stitch to form flowers:

ROUND 1: Use 4' (122 cm) of thread to string {1D and 1A} five times, leaving a 6" (15 cm) tail. Tie a square knot with the tail and working threads to form a circle. Exit the first bead added (**fig. 1, blue**).

ROUND 2: String 2B, skip the nearest A, and pass through the following D to form the first circular peyote stitch; repeat four times to add a total of 10B (**fig. 1, red**). *Note:* Step up for this and each subsequent round by passing through the first bead added in the current round.

ROUND 3: String 2B, pass down through the next B of Round 2 (this forms the first herringbone stitch), string 1C, and pass up through the following B of Round 2; repeat four times to add a total of 10B and 5C (**fig. 2**).

ROUND 4: String 2B; pass down through the next B of Round 3. String 1C, 1A, and 1C; pass up through the following B of Round 3. Repeat from the beginning of this round four times to add a total of 10B, 10C, and 5A (**fig. 3**).

ROUND 5: String 1B, 1A, and 1B; pass down through the next B of Round 4 and the following C of Round 4 to form a picot. String 1C, 1A, and 1C; pass through the next C of Round 4 and up through the following B of Round 4 to form a picot (**fig. 4, blue**). Repeat from the beginning of this round four times to add a total of 10B, 10A, and 10C (**fig. 4, red**). Secure the thread but don't trim. Set aside.

Repeat this entire step eleven times for a total of twelve single-layer flowers.

2 Two-layer flowers.

Use circular herringbone stitch to form two-layer flowers:

Repeat Step 1, Rounds 1–5 using 5' (152.5 cm) of thread and leaving a 10" (25.5 cm) tail; don't trim the working thread. Weave the tail thread clockwise through beads to exit the right side of 1D of Round 1. *Note:* You'll now begin working clockwise.

ROUND 6: String 2C and pass through the next D of Round 1; repeat four times to add a total of 10C (**fig. 5, blue**). *Note:* Step up for this and each subsequent round by passing through the first bead added in the current round.

ROUND 7: String 1C, 1A, and 1C; pass down through the next C of Round 6 to form a picot. String 2A; pass through the following C of Round 6. Repeat from the beginning of this round four times to add a total of 15A and 10C (**fig. 5, red**). Secure the thread and trim. Set aside.

Repeat this entire step ten times for a total of eleven two-layer flowers.

3 Clasp.

Form a clasp using flowers, Ultrasuede, and the snap set:

PREP: Separate the snap, trace around each half onto a piece of Ultrasuede, and trim the Ultrasuede to the size of the snap.

BOTTOM: Weave the thread of one single-layer flower through beads to exit a bead of Round 2. Center one circle of Ultrasuede on top of the flower, then center the male half of the snap over the circle of Ultrasuede. Sew the snap to the flower, passing through the Ultrasuede and the beads of Rounds 1 and 2 (**fig. 6**). Be sure to pass through each hole of the snap several times.

TOP: Using the same technique as for the bottom, attach the female half of the snap and the remaining circle of Ultrasuede on the underside of one double-layer flower.

4 Assembly. Weave the thread of one single-layer flower through beads to exit 1A of Round 5 that sits between 2B, pass through 1A of Round 5 that sits between 2B on a double-layer flower, and pass through the first A exited on the single-layer flower again to form a square stitch (**fig. 7, blue**). Repeat the thread path twice to reinforce. Secure the thread and trim.

Weave the thread of the double-layer flower just added through beads to exit 1A of Round 5 that sits between 2B and is opposite the last one connected. *Note:* There should be one long petal made of B between the last one connected and the one you're now exiting. Square-stitch the A last exited to 1A of Round 5 that sits between 2B on a new single-layer flower (**fig. 7, red**).

Continue connecting flowers in the same manner, alternating single- and double-layer flowers, beginning and ending with a clasp half, ensuring all double-layer flowers are faceup, and orienting the flowers so they point up as in **fig. 7**. *Note:* The single-layer snap half will connect to a single-layer flower at one end.

TIPS

- Make sure the square-stitch connections formed in Step 4 are strong and reinforced or your necklace could come apart.

- You can omit the Ultrasuede circles on the snap connection, but having them makes it easier to sew the snap to the beadwork.

- To accentuate the dimension of the two-layer flowers, work the top layer (Rounds 6 and 7) in a contrasting color.

- Replace the size 15°s at the tip of select petals with 2mm crystals for extra sparkle. If you opt for this, place the crystals only at the tips of the bottom layer's short petals and the top layer's petals so that you're still connecting seed bead to seed bead in Step 4.

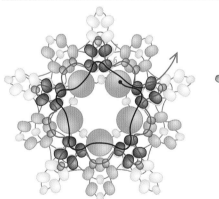

fig. 5: working rounds 6 and 7

fig. 6: adding half of the snap to one single-layer flower

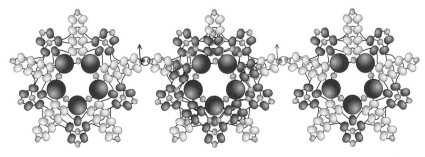

fig. 7: square-stitching the flowers together

DESIGN OPTION

BY MELINDA BARTA

Create the look of petals by working the long herringbone columns of Rounds 1–5 in graduating shades of green (instead of silver). Work the other loops and picots in red and purple hues (instead of dark purple) to look like flower petals.

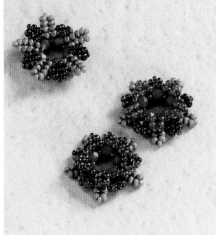

DESIGN OPTION

Rose Garden Necklace

BY MELINDA BARTA

This necklace pairs the two-layer floral components (page 60) of the Graceful Garland necklace with smaller six-petal components. The elements are joined with jump rings and finished with dainty brass chain and vintage dangles. Small crystal teardrop pendants would also look great hanging from the central components.

MATERIALS

0.5 g matte metallic copper bronze iris size 15° Japanese seed beads (A)

0.5 g metallic gold/bronze iris size 15° Japanese seed beads (B)

1 g matte metallic copper bronze iris size 11° Japanese seed beads (C)

1 g matte metallic antique rose size 11° Japanese seed beads (D)

1 g mauve permanent galvanized size 11° Japanese seed beads (E)

24 milky rose/bronze Vega 3mm fire-polished rounds (F)

3 brass with matte glass 5×12mm rectangle dangles

1 natural brass 10×22mm swirl hook-and-eye clasp

7 brass 4.5mm jump rings

7 brass 6mm jump rings

14¾" (37.5 cm) of natural brass 4×6mm ladder chain

Smoke 6 lb braided beading thread

TOOLS

Scissors

Size 12 needle

Wire cutters

2 pairs of chain- or flat-nose pliers

FINISHED SIZE

19" (48.5 cm)

fig. A

fig. B

fig. C

fig. D

1 TWO-LAYER FLOWER, CENTER. Repeat Step 2 for the Graceful Garland necklace (page 60): In Round 1, use F and B. In Round 2, use E. In Round 3, work 2E between each 2E pair of Round 2 and 2A over each F of Round 1. In Round 4, work 2E between each 2E pair of Round 3 and 1C/1A/1C over each 2A set of Round 3. In Round 5, work 1E/1B/1E between each 2E pair of Round 4 and 1C/1A/1C over each A of Round 4. In Round 6, use D. In Round 7, use 1D/1B/1D between each 2D pair of Round 6 and 2B over each F of Round 1. Set aside.

2 TWO-LAYER FLOWERS, SIDES. Repeat Step 1 above, but in Round 1 use A in place of B. Repeat to form a second two-layer flower; these will be placed on each side of the flower formed in Step 1. Set aside.

3 SIX-PETAL FLOWERS.

Use circular peyote and circular herringbone stitches to form small, six-petal flowers:

ROUND 1: Use 3' (91.5 cm) of thread to string {1F and 1B} three times, leaving a 6" (15 cm) tail. Tie a knot to form a circle and pass through the first bead strung **(fig. A, blue)**.

ROUND 2: String 2E, skip the nearest B, and pass through the next F to form the first circular peyote stitch; repeat twice to add a total of 6E **(fig. A, red)**. *Note:* Step up for this and each subsequent round by passing through the first bead added in the current round.

ROUND 3: String 1E, 1B, and 1E, then pass through the next E of Round 2; repeat five times to add a total of 12E and 6B. Weave through beads to exit the third E added in this round, above an F of Round 1 **(fig. B, blue)**.

ROUND 4: String 3B and pass through the next E of Round 3 to form a picot, then weave through beads to exit the next E of Round 3 above an F; repeat. String 3B; pass through the following E of Round 3 and the nearest E of Round 2 **(fig. B, red)**.

ROUND 5: String 1A; pass through the next E of Round 2. *Note:* This A should align with the B of Round 1. String 5A; pass through the following E of Round 2. *Note:* The 5A should wrap around the F of Round 1. Repeat from the beginning of this round twice to add a total of 18A **(fig. C)**. Secure the thread and trim. Set aside.

Repeat this entire step for a second metallic bronze/mauve six-petal flower.

Repeat this entire step using C in place of E in Rounds 2–4 and B in place of A in Round 5 to form a matte cabernet six-petal flower.

4 ASSEMBLY.

Use one 4.5mm jump ring to attach one half of the clasp to one end of one 7¼" (18.5 cm) piece of chain; repeat using the other half of the clasp, making sure the loops of the decorative chain will point in the same direction when worn.

Connect the flowers, dangles, and chain ends as indicated in **fig. D**, using 6mm (shown in red) and 4.5mm jump rings (shown in blue). Pass the jump rings through the flower petal loops; gently open the loops with chain-nose pliers if needed.

Bezel a shimmering set of crystal chatons framed in eight-pointed stars using a circular herringbone stitch. Netted connections adorned with crystals and picot embellishments complete this graceful accessory. • *by Kelly Wiese*

starbright bracelet

TECHNIQUES

Circular herringbone stitch

Flat and circular peyote stitch

Netting

Picot

Square stitch

Zipping

MATERIALS

5 g silver-lined teal AB size 15° Japanese seed beads (A)

3 g metallic bronze size 15° Japanese seed beads (B)

8 g metallic bronze size 11° Japanese seed beads (C)

12 blue zircon 3mm crystal bicones

14 blue zircon 4mm crystal bicones

7 blue zircon SS29 (about 6mm) pointed-back faceted round crystal chatons

Brown size D nylon beading thread

Thread conditioner

TOOLS

Scissors

Size 12 beading needles

FINISHED SIZE

7½" (19 cm)

1 **Stars.** Use circular peyote and herringbone stitches to bezel crystal chatons into star-shaped components:

ROUNDS 1 AND 2: Use 4' (122 cm) of thread to string {1A and 1C} eight times to add a total of 8A and 8C. Pass through all of the beads again to form a circle. Exit the first C added (**fig. 1, blue**).

ROUND 3: String 1C, skip 1A of Round 1, and pass through the next C of Round 2 to form the first circular peyote stitch; repeat seven times to add a total of 8C (**fig. 1, red**). *Note:* Unless otherwise noted, step up for this and each subsequent round by passing through the first bead added in the current round.

ROUND 4: String 2C and pass through the next C of Round 3; repeat seven times to add a total of 16C (**fig. 2, blue**).

ROUND 5: String 2C, then pass down through the next C of Round 4 and up through the following C of Round 4 (this forms the first herringbone stitch); repeat seven times to add a total of 16C (**fig. 2, red**).

ROUND 6: String 1C; pass down through the next C of Round 5. String 1C; skip over the next column of C and pass up through the following C of Round 5 (**fig. 3, blue**). Pull snug. *Note:* In this round, every other herringbone column will pull up to form the back of the bezel; push the others down toward your work surface.

Repeat from the beginning of this round three times to add a total of 8C (**fig. 3, red**).

ROUND 7: Insert 1 chaton into the bezel facedown with its face touching Rounds 1–3. Hold the chaton in place as you work this round. String 1C, skip 1C of Round 6, and pass through the next C of Round 6; repeat three times to add a total of 4C (**fig. 4, blue**). Retrace the thread path of this round to reinforce. Weave through beads to exit a C of Round 3, toward one of the herringbone columns that's sticking out away from the bezel (**fig. 4, red**). Turn the bezel over; you will now begin working clockwise around the front of the bezel. Secure the tail thread and trim.

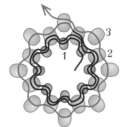

fig. 1: forming rounds 1–3

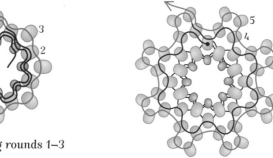

fig. 2: adding rounds 4 and 5

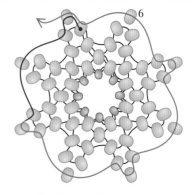

fig. 3: working round 6

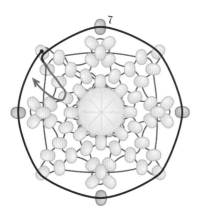

fig. 4: stitching round 7 and stepping up for round 8

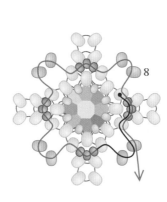

fig. 5: adding round 8

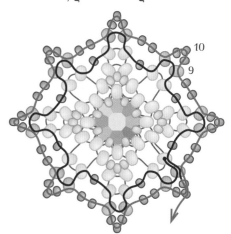

fig. 6: stitching rounds 9 and 10

ROUND 8: String 3A; pass through the next C of Round 3 to form a picot. String 2C; pass through the next C of Round 3 (**fig. 5, blue**). Repeat from the beginning of this round three times to add a total of 12A and 8C. Weave through beads to step up through the first C added in this round (**fig. 5, red**).

ROUND 9: String 2C; pass down through the next C of Round 8. String 1A; pass up through the following C of Round 5. String 2C; pass down through the next C of Round 5. String 1A; pass up through the following C of Round 8. Repeat from the beginning of this round three times to add a total of 16C and 8A (**fig. 6, blue**). *Note:* This round creates 4 new herringbone columns between the 4 original columns that weren't folded up to form the bezel.

ROUND 10: String 3A, pass down through the next C of Round 9 to form a picot, then string 2A and pass up through the following C of Round 9; repeat seven times to add a total of 40A. Step up through the first 2A added in this round (**fig. 6, red**). Don't trim the thread. Set aside.
Repeat this entire step six times for a total of seven stars.

2 Connections. Join the bezeled components with short strands:

LEFT SIDE: Using the working thread from one star, string 3B, one 3mm bicone, and 3B, then pass down through the middle A of the next Round 10 picot on the same star; repeat (**fig. 7, blue**).

BOTTOM: String 3B, one 4mm bicone, and 3B; pass up through the middle A of a Round 10 picot on a second star. String 3B; pass back through the second 3mm bicone added in this step (**fig. 7, red**). *Note:* Make sure both stars are faceup.

RIGHT SIDE: String 3B; pass up through the middle A of the next Round 10 picot on the second star. Square-stitch the two stars together, passing through the touching As of Round 10 (**fig. 8, green**). String 3B; pass back through the first 3mm bicone added in this step (**fig. 8, blue**).

TOP: String 3B; pass up through the middle A of the next Round 10 picot on the second star. String 3B, one 4mm bicone, and 3B; pass through the first A exited in this step (**fig. 8, red**). Retrace the thread path of the entire connection to reinforce. Secure the thread and trim.
Repeat this entire step five times to connect the five remaining stars end to end.

TIPS

- If the chatons seem a little loose in the bezels, help tighten and reinforce the beadwork by retracing the thread paths of Rounds 5–7.

- For a simpler bracelet, omit the connections formed in Step 2 and join the tips of the stars' longer herringbone columns.

- To turn an individual star into an earring, add a decorative crystal or glass drop bead to one long herringbone column and an ear wire to the opposite column; repeat to complete the pair of earrings. Wear just one star as a pendant.

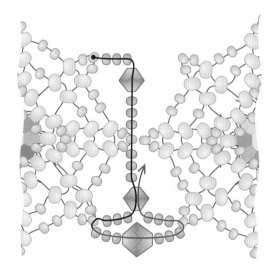

fig. 7: working the left-side and bottom connections

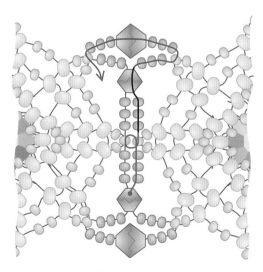

fig. 8: forming the right-side and top connections

3 Toggle bar. Use flat peyote stitch to make a toggle bar and attach it to one end of the bracelet:

TUBE: Use 3' (91.5 cm) of new thread to work a strip of flat peyote stitch 22B wide and 8 rows long, leaving a 6" (15 cm) tail. Fold the strip so the first and last rows interlock. Zip the beads together to form a seamless tube **(fig. 9)**. Exit through the end of the tube.

ENDS: String one 4mm bicone and 3B; pass back through the 4mm bicone to form a picot. Pass through the center of the tube to exit the other end **(fig. 10, green)**. Repeat this section to add another 4mm bicone and 3B picot to the other end of the tube. Repeat the thread path at both ends to reinforce. Weave through beads to exit the twelfth B from one end of the tube **(fig. 10, blue)**.

ATTACH: String 6B; pass through the middle A of the Round 10 picot at one end of the bracelet. String 6B; pass through the eleventh B from one end of the tube and the last B exited on the tube **(fig. 10, red)**. Repeat the thread path several times to reinforce. Secure the thread and trim.

4 Clasp loop. Use circular peyote stitch to form the clasp loop:

ROUNDS 1 AND 2: Turn the work around so the end opposite the toggle bar points up. Start 12" (30.5 cm) of new thread that exits the middle A of the Round 10 picot at the end of the bracelet. String 29B; pass through the last A exited and the first B just strung **(fig. 11, blue)**.

ROUND 3: String 1B, skip 1B previously strung, and pass through the next B; repeat to add a total of 14B **(fig. 11, red)**. Secure the thread and trim.

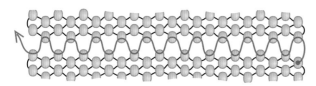

fig. 9: zipping the peyote tube

fig. 10: embellishing the ends of the toggle bar and attaching it to the bracelet

fig. 11: beading the clasp loop

DESIGN OPTIONS

BY KELLY WIESE

- Play with color! Kelly's timeless combination of cream-and-gold seed beads with topaz crystals is perfect for a bride, an anniversary party, or any other special occasion.

- Purple crystals with gold/bronze iris and purple seed beads give the bracelet a sweet look for spring or summer.

The combination of long, swooping chains with asymmetrical clusters of flower-shaped beaded charms makes this modern necklace irresistible. Soft pink, gold, purple, and silver-hued seed beads with matte-finish chain create a feminine look. ● *by Melinda Barta*

gilded blossoms

TECHNIQUES

Circular herringbone stitch

Circular and tubular peyote stitch

Wireworking

MATERIALS

0.5 g matte metallic cabernet iris size 15° Japanese seed beads (A)

0.5 g silver-lined light gray size 15° Japanese seed beads

0.5 g 24k gold electroplate size 15° Japanese seed beads

0.5 g mocha berry opaque size 15° Japanese seed beads

1 g semifrost dark mauve galvanized size 11° cylinder beads (B)

0.5 g light amethyst galvanized size 11° cylinder beads (C)

1 g semimatte galvanized pewter size 11° cylinder beads

0.5 g galvanized pewter size 11° cylinder beads

1 g semifrost honey wine galvanized size 11° cylinder beads

0.5 g bright gold galvanized size 11° cylinder beads

3 g semimatte golden copper galvanized size 11° cylinder beads (D)

2 g golden copper galvanized size 11° cylinder beads (E)

1 g matte pink blush galvanized size 11° cylinder beads

0.5 g silver-lined English rose opal size 11° cylinder beads

1 g matte plum wine galvanized size 11° cylinder beads

0.5 g metallic berry/gold rainbow size 11° cylinder beads

13 matte transparent light topaz AB size 8° seed beads (F)

1 gold-plated 7×12mm lobster clasp

1 brass 24-gauge 2½" (6.5 cm) head pin with 3mm ball end

20 matte silver-plated 4mm (outer diameter)/3mm (inner diameter) jump rings

1 matte silver-plated 6mm (outer diameter)/5mm (inner diameter) jump ring

36¼" (92 cm) of matte gold base-metal 2.5mm rolo chain

36⅞" (93.7 cm) of matte gold base-metal 1.5×2mm oval chain with sections of larger oval links (2×3mm) and 3mm ball links

38¾" (98.5 cm) of matte silver base-metal 2mm rolo chain

37½" (95 cm) of matte silver base-metal 1.5×2mm oval chain with sections of larger oval links (2×3mm) and 3mm ball links

37¼" (94.5 cm) of matte black base-metal 1.5×2mm oval chain with sections of larger oval links (2×3mm) and 3mm ball links

Smoke 6 lb braided beading thread

Tan One-G nylon beading thread

TOOLS

Scissors

Size 10 and 12 beading needles

Wire cutters

Round-nose pliers

2 pairs of chain- or flat-nose pliers

Chopstick

FINISHED SIZE

36¾" (93.5 cm)

NOTE

Start with the size 10 needle and switch to the size 12 when noted, or any time you have trouble fitting the needle through beads.

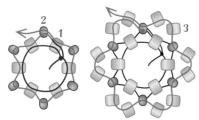

fig. 1: forming rounds 1 and 2

fig. 2: adding round 3

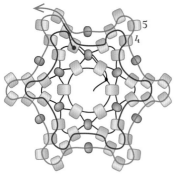

fig. 3: stitching rounds 4 and 5

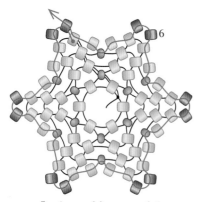

fig. 4: working round 6

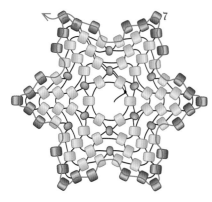

fig. 5: adding round 7

1 Flower front. Use circular herringbone and circular peyote stitches to form the front half of a flower:

ROUND 1: Use 4' (122 cm) of smoke thread to string 6B, leaving an 8" (20.5 cm) tail. Pass through all of the beads again and tie a square knot with the tail and working threads to form a circle. Exit the first bead added, making sure the knot doesn't slip inside the bead **(fig. 1, blue).**

ROUND 2: String 1A and pass through the next B of Round 1 to form the first circular peyote stitch; repeat five times to add a total of 6A **(fig. 1, red).** *Note:* Step up for this and each subsequent round by passing through the first bead added in the current round.

ROUND 3: String 2B and pass through the next A of Round 2; repeat five times to add a total of 12B **(fig. 2).**

ROUND 4: String 2B, then pass down through the next B of Round 3 and up through the following B of Round 3 (this forms the first herringbone stitch); repeat five times to add a total of 12B **(fig. 3, blue).**

ROUND 5: String 2B, pass through the next B of Round 4, string 1A, and pass up through the following B of Round 4; repeat five times to add a total of 12B and 6A **(fig. 3, red).**

ROUND 6: String 2C; pass through the next B of Round 5. String 1B; pass through the nearest A of Round 5. String 1B; pass up through the following B of Round 5. *Note:* This forms 2 circular peyote stitches between the herringbone columns. Repeat from the

beginning of this round five times to add a total of 12C and 12B **(fig. 4).**

ROUND 7: String 1C; pass through the next C of Round 6. String 1C; pass through the following 2B of Round 6. String 1C; pass up through the next C of Round 6. Repeat from the beginning of this round five times to add a total of 18C **(fig. 5).** Secure the working and tail threads and trim. Set aside.

2 Flower back. Use circular herringbone and circular peyote stitches to form the back half of a flower:

FLOWER: Repeat Rounds 1–6 of Step 1 using B in place of A; don't trim the threads.

ZIPPING: Work Round 7 as before, but instead of stringing new C beads, pass through those added in Step 1, Round 7 on the flower front to zip the 2 halves together **(fig. 6).** Notice that as you zip the front and back together, in some places you pass through a single bead and in some places a pair of beads along the edge in order to follow the thread path of Round 7. Manipulate the beadwork so the flower front is concave. Secure the thread and trim.

ANCHOR BEAD: Add a size 12 needle to the tail thread and pass through the nearest B of Round 1. String 1F; pass through the B of Round 1 that's opposite the one last exited. Pass back through the F and through the first B exited **(fig. 7).** Repeat the thread path twice. *Note:* It's helpful to use the skinniest of the F beads you can find because you'll later be passing jump rings through these beads, and wide F beads can make the jump ring hard to close. Secure the thread and trim. Set the dark mauve flower aside.

3 Remaining flower charms. Make additional flower charms with the following color changes:

DARK MAUVE: Repeat Steps 1 and 2 for a second dark mauve flower charm.

SILVER: Repeat Steps 1 and 2 twice using gray size 15°s in place of A, semimatte pewter size 11°s in place of B, and pewter (not semimatte) size 11°s in place of C for a total of two silver flower charms.

LIGHT GOLD: Repeat Steps 1 and 2 twice using gold size 15°s in place of A, semifrost honey wine size 11°s in place of B, and bright gold size 11°s in place of C for a total of two light gold flower charms.

GOLDEN COPPER: Repeat Steps 1 and 2 three times using gold size 15°s in place of A, D in place of B, and E in place of C for a total of three golden copper flower charms; omit the anchor bead on the third flower (this will form the clasp dangle).

LIGHT PINK: Repeat Steps 1 and 2 using mocha berry size 15°s in place of A, matte pink blush size 11°s in place of B, and silver-lined English rose opal size 11°s in place of C for a total of two light pink flower charms.

DARK PINK: Repeat Steps 1 and 2 using mocha berry size 15°s in place of A, matte plum wine size 11°s in place of B, and metallic berry/gold rainbow size 11°s in place of C for a total of two dark pink flower charms.

4 Collars. If desired, make tubular-peyote collars to surround the chain above and below the charm sections:

ROUNDS 1 AND 2: Use 18" (45.5 cm) of tan thread to string 16D, leaving a 9" (23 cm) tail. Pass through the first 4 beads again; don't tie a knot. Slide the ring over the chopstick (**fig. 8, green**). *Note:* While beading the following rounds, pull firmly on the tail and working threads while beading to maintain tight tension. Working around a chopstick and maintaining tight tension keeps the tube from collapsing onto itself.

ROUND 3: String 1D, skip 1D previously strung, and pass

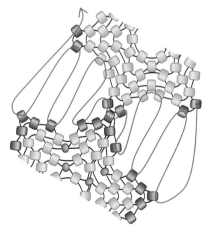

fig. 6: zipping the flower back to the front

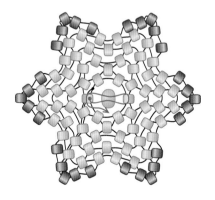

fig. 7: adding the anchor bead

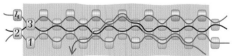

fig. 8: working rounds 1–4 of the collar

through the next D; repeat seven times to add a total of 8D (**fig. 8, blue**). *Note:* Unless otherwise noted, step up for this and each subsequent round by passing through the first bead added in the current round.

ROUND 4: Work 8 stitches with 1E in each stitch to add a total of 8E. Weave through beads to exit a D of Round 1 (**fig. 8, red**).

ROUNDS 5 AND 6: Work 1D in each stitch to add a total of 8D in each of 2 rounds (**fig. 9, blue**).

ROUND 7: Work 8 stitches with 1E in each stitch to add a total of 8E (**fig. 9, red**). Weave through beads to exit a D of Round 1; don't trim the working thread. Add a needle to the tail thread and weave through any rounds that need tightening; secure the tail thread and trim. Remove the chopstick and set the collar aside.

Repeat this entire step three times for a total of four collars.

5 **Chain assembly.** Join the chains and attach the collars:

CHAIN ENDS: Attach the 6mm jump ring to one end of each chain. *Note:* If you have trouble passing the jump ring through any of the final chain links, use flat-nose pliers to gently squeeze the ends of the links toward each other, slightly opening the link. Use 6" (15 cm) of smoke thread to string the final links at the other end of the chains; tie a square knot with the tail and working threads to form a small loop (**fig. 10, blue**). Use 6" (15 cm) of smoke thread to form another small loop that joins the one just made to the 6mm jump ring (**fig. 10, red**). *Note:* This smoke thread is temporary and will be removed later when adding the clasp dangle.

JOIN CHAINS: Hang the chains on a bulletin board, knob of a kitchen cabinet, or anywhere else that allows the chains to hang freely with the ends at the center top. Smooth the chains so they aren't excessively twisted. They should hang straight and side by side in this upper portion of the necklace; the difference in chain length is only seen at the bottom center of the necklace. Measure down 7⅛" (18.3 cm) from the chain ends on the left side of the necklace and attach one 4mm jump ring to the chains, passing through as many chain links as possible. For the chains with links too small to conveniently string, just make sure they pass through the center of the jump ring when closed. Repeat to join the chains with a second 4mm jump ring 2⅛" (5.3 cm) below the last one placed. Measure down 8⅝" (21.5 cm) from the chain ends on the right side of the necklace and attach one 4mm jump ring to the chains as before. Add a fourth 4mm jump ring 2⅝" (6.5 cm) below the one just placed.

TACK COLLARS: Cut the second loop of smoke thread (indicated

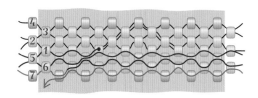

fig. 9: stitching rounds 5–7 of the collar

fig. 10: creating temporary thread loops on the chain ends

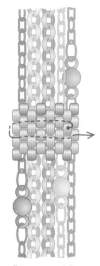

fig. 11: tacking a collar to the chains

in red in **fig. 10**). Use the end of the chains with the 6mm jump ring to string one collar; slide it down over the bottom 4mm jump ring added on the left side of the necklace. Use the collar's working thread to pass through the center of the collar and several chain links and exit the opposite side of the collar. Pass through the nearest bead of Round 1. Pass back through the center of the collar, through several chain links, and through the first bead exited on the collar (**fig. 11**). Weave through a few beads of Rounds 1 and 2 and repeat the thread path several times to reinforce and secure the tube in place. *Note:* Don't use tight tension or you'll distort the collar. Hold your needle straight when passing through the center of the collar and chain links to keep the collar straight in line with the chains. Secure the thread and trim. Use the end of the chains with the 6mm jump ring to string a second collar and slide it down over the top 4mm jump ring added on the left side of the necklace. Repeat this entire section on the right side of the necklace; don't trim the first loop of the smoke thread.

6 **Finishing.** Complete the clasps and attach the flower charms:

LOBSTER: Open the 6mm jump ring, string the lobster clasp, and then close the jump ring.

CLASP DANGLE: Cut the first loop of smoke thread (indicated in blue in **fig. 10**). Use the head pin to string the golden copper flower without the anchor bead (front to back) from Step 3. String 1F and form a large

(about 5 mm) wrapped loop that attaches to the free chain ends (**fig. 12**). *Note:* The loop of the dangle needs to be large enough to accommodate the chain ends and, when the necklace is worn, the lobster clasp.

FLOWER CHARMS: Rehang the necklace as before and use 4mm jump rings to attach the F of five flower charms between the collars on the left side of the necklace; repeat to add the seven remaining flower charms between the collars on the right side of the necklace. Space the flower charms evenly along the chain sections and arrange the colors to your liking, or refer to the photo above. To keep the flower charms from drooping

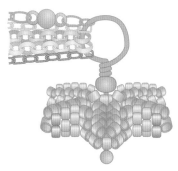

fig. 12: forming the clasp dangle

and pulling the chains out of place, pass through as many chain links as possible. For the chains with links too small to conveniently pass a jump ring through, position the chains so they hang inside the center of the jump ring when closed.

TIPS

- The easiest way to measure and cut chain is to hang it in front of a yardstick. When working with chains that have a mix of different-sized links (like the oval-and-ball chain used in this project), plan your cuts so that the chain starts and ends with the largest of the links.

- Instead of using a 6mm jump ring, use 5" (12.5 cm) of 24-gauge wire to make a wire-wrapped link that attaches the chains to the lobster clasp. This is helpful if you have trouble stringing the chain ends with the jump ring.

- One-G brand nylon beading thread works better than Nymo brand for the peyote collars because its slight stretchiness helps make the collars tight and round.

DESIGN OPTION

Chocolate Flower Earrings

BY MELINDA BARTA

To make these beautiful, romantic earrings, bead five-petal flowers to layer on top of the six-petal flowers featured in Gilded Blossoms (page 70). Finish them with faceted smoky quartz teardrops.

MATERIALS

0.5 g burgundy size 13° charlottes (A)

0.5 g matte metallic copper iris size 11° cylinder beads (B)

0.5 g metallic copper gold iris size 11° cylinder beads (C)

2 smoky quartz 6×19mm faceted top-drilled teardrops

1 pair of brass 10×20mm ear wires

Smoke 6 lb beading thread

TOOLS

Scissors

Size 12 and 13 beading needles

2 pairs of chain- or flat-nose pliers

FINISHED SIZE

1⅛" (4.7 cm)

1 SIX-PETAL FLOWER. Repeat Step 1 for the Gilded Blossoms necklace (page 72) using burgundy size 13° charlottes for A, matte metallic copper iris size 11° cylinder beads for B, and metallic (not matte) copper gold iris size 11° cylinder beads for C. Secure the thread and trim. Set aside.

2 FIVE-PETAL FLOWER. Repeat Step 1 for the Gilded Blossoms necklace, but in Round 1, string {1B and 1A} only five times. Each of the following rounds will have one fewer repeat, forming a flower with five petals.

DANGLE: Exiting a C of Round 7 at the tip of a flower petal, string 5A, the teardrop, and 5A. Pass through the tip of the flower petal again to form a dangle. Repeat the thread path at least once. *Note:* You may need to switch to a smaller needle to pass through the size 15°s and the stone teardrop.

3 ASSEMBLY. Join the flowers and add an ear wire:

FLOWERS: Weave the thread of the five-petal flower through beads to exit a B of Round 1. Connect the Round 1 beads of this flower to the Round 1 beads of the six-petal flower. *Note:* Orient the six-petal flower so one petal is opposite the five-petal flower's dangle (the ear wire will connect to this top petal). Secure the thread and trim.

EAR WIRE: Opening and closing the loop of the ear wire as you would a jump ring, connect the ear wire to the top petal of the six-petal flower, passing through the opening below the top 3 beads (the tip bead of Round 7 and the 2C of Round 6).

4 REPEAT Steps 1–3 above for a second earring.

tubular herringbone stitch

Like circular herringbone, tubular herringbone stitch is worked in the round. However, the beads of tubular herringbone stack to form dimensional objects such as ropes, beaded beads, bangles, and much more. Spice up tubular herringbone with these fun variations and embellishments.

Tubular herringbone stitch doesn't have to always be tubular. In my **Tambourine Bangles**, I show you how working in the round can actually create two flat surfaces. Plus, learn to sandwich decorative accent beads within these sturdy layers.

Make three different sizes of beaded beads with tubular herringbone stitch, plus stylish matching ropes finished with leather and wire, in my **Hawthorne Necklace**. Contrast the highly textured surface of the beaded beads with smooth and shiny lampwork beads.

Give odd-count tubular herringbone stitch a try in my **Constellations Necklace**. Three ropes, each with subtle hints of sparkle from tiny crystal bicones, are joined by decorative collars beaded with tubular herringbone and adorned with crystals. Also see my variation on the design, **Roped In Necklace**.

TECHNIQUES

counting

Count rounds of tubular herringbone stitch just as you would rounds of circular herringbone stitch. See page 55 for more information on counting columns and accent beads.

illustrations

It's common to see this stitch illustrated both in the round, from a bird's-eye view (as seen in **fig. 1**), and as a flat side view (as seen in **fig. 2**). Flat side views typically show all the beads in the round, meaning the threads that end on the left side of the illustration connect to the threads on the right side of the illustration. You may find a combination of both styles in the same project because it's often easier to stitch the first few rounds with a bird's-eye-view perspective. Regardless of how a piece is illustrated, always be mindful of the step-ups at the end of each round.

even-count tubular herringbone stitch

Establish Round 1 by ladder-stitching an even number of beads; stitch the first and last beads together to form a ring, exiting up through a bead (**figs. 3** and **4, blue;** both bird's-eye and side views shown).

For Round 2, string 2 beads, pass down through the next bead of the previous round and up through the following bead. Repeat around and step up by passing through the first bead added in this round (**figs. 3** and **4, red;** both bird's-eye and side views shown). This step-up is very important. Work with tight tension to encourage the beadwork to form a tube. You may

find it helpful to insert a chopstick, small dowel, crochet hook, or knitting needle at this point and work the next few rounds around the armature until the structure is established.

Repeat Round 2 to continue working the tube of beadwork. Notice the step-ups at the end of each round; each thread color in **fig. 5** indicates a new round. To close the end of the rope, see Ending Tubes on page 81.

Alternate step-ups cause the beadwork to twist and spiral—see these interesting variations starting on page 103.

odd-count tubular herringbone stitch

Give this variation of tubular herringbone a try. Work Round 1 by ladder-stitching a strip 1 bead high and 3 beads long; stitch the first and last beads together to form a ring.

For the first stitch of Round 2, string 2 beads; pass down through the next bead of the previous round and up through the following bead of the previous round (**figs. 6** and **7, blue;** both bird's-eye and side views shown). For the second stitch of this round, string 1 bead; pass down through the first bead of this round and the nearest bead of the previous round, then pass up through the next bead of the previous round and the second bead added in this round (**figs. 6** and **7, red;** both bird's-eye and side views shown).

Repeat Round 2 for the desired length.

To work this with 4 beads in the first stitch, 2 beads in the second stitch, and accent beads interspersed, see my **Constellations Necklace** on page 96.

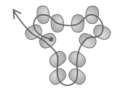

fig. 1

fig. 2

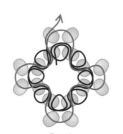

fig. 3

fig. 4

fig. 5

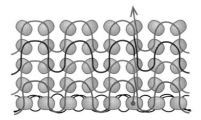

fig. 6   fig. 7

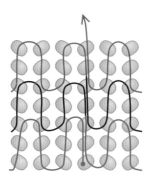

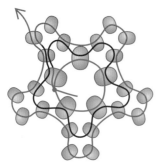

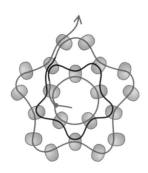

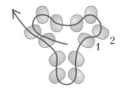

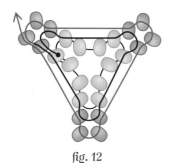

fig. 8

fig. 9

fig. 10

fig. 11

fig. 12

two-drop tubular herringbone stitch

Work each round with twice as many beads to rapidly grow the work. Simply work 4 beads in each stitch instead of 2. When stepping up at the end of the round, be sure to pass up through the first 2 beads of the first stitch (**fig. 8**).

alternate starts

Although starting with a ladder-stitched ring of beads has become the most popular way to start tubular herringbone, here are a few alternatives:

RING OF BEADS

Form a small ring of beads for Round 1 and exit the first bead strung (**fig. 9, green**). In Round 2, work 2 beads between each bead of Round 1; step up through the first bead of this round (**fig. 9, blue**). Begin tubular herringbone as usual in Round 3 (**fig. 9, red**). Use tight tension and the tube will begin to take shape after 4 herringbone rounds are worked. Play around with the size of Round 1 beads to control the size of the opening. This works best using size 6° or size 8° seed beads for Round 1 and size 11° seed beads for the following rounds.

CIRCULAR PEYOTE STITCH

If making the tube with all the same size beads, such as all size 11°s, start with a small ring of circular peyote stitch: Form a small ring of beads for Round 1 and exit the first bead strung (**fig. 10, green**). In Round 2, work 1 bead between each bead of Round 1; step up through the first bead of this round (**fig. 10, blue**). Work Round 3 with 2 beads between each bead of Round 2; step up through the first bead of this round (**fig. 10, red**). Begin tubular herringbone as usual in Round 4.

STACKED START

Also sometimes called a "traditional" start, this method is quick, avoids the sometimes rigid nature of a ladder-stitch start, and adds the beads of both Rounds 1 and 2 at the same time. As you add the beads of Round 3, the beads of the starting ring stack to form Rounds 1 and 2. Have patience, because this method can seem difficult at first, but it is well worth the effort. Learn the technique by following this sample. When playing around with your own variations, determine the number of beads needed for Rounds 1 and 2 by multiplying the number of columns you want in your tube by 4. Here, a 3-column tube is formed by stringing 12 beads for Rounds 1 and 2.

ROUNDS 1 AND 2: String 12 beads, leaving a tail at least 8" (20.5 cm) long. Pass through the first 2 beads strung; don't tie a knot (**fig. 11**).

ROUND 3: String 2 beads, pass down through the next bead of the starting ring, skip over 2 beads, and then pass through the next bead; repeat twice to add a total of 6 beads. Step up by passing through the first bead added in this round (**fig. 12, blue**). *Note:* Pull back on the tail as you work this and the following rounds to encourage the beads to stack.

ROUND 4: String 2 beads, pass down through the next bead in the current column, and pass up through the first bead in the following column; repeat twice to add a total of 6 beads (**fig. 12, red**). Continue in tubular herringbone as usual.

Work this technique in my **Hawthorne Necklace** (page 90) and **Constellations Necklace** (page 96).

BRICK STITCH

When beading around a cabochon or other focal that's attached to a beading foundation, work the first round with an even number of brick stitches (page 135) to properly orient the beads for the following herringbone rounds.

ending tubes

There are many ways to close the end of a tubular herringbone rope. Here are two stitched methods. To cleanly cover the ends with caps, see the Finishing Beaded Ropes section on page 83.

RING

Form a small ring at the end by passing through all beads of the final round several times (fig. 13).

LADDER STITCH

Join the beads of the final round with a ladder-stitch thread path (fig. 14).

PEYOTE STITCH

Work the final round with 3 beads in each stitch to form a picot at the top of each column (fig. 15, green). Or, work another round with 1 bead in each stitch. To begin closing the end, peyote-stitch 1 bead between the tip bead of each column (the center bead of each 3-bead picot in the final round) (fig. 15, blue). To close the end, pass through each bead added in the previous round (fig. 15, red).

accent beads

Here's my favorite part of tubular herringbone stitch—embellishments! Dress up herringbone with easy-to-add accent beads, place them between columns, or work them right into a column.

BETWEEN-COLUMN ACCENTS

Add accent beads between columns of tubular herringbone just as you did in the flat herringbone technique section (page 29). Be sure to step up through the first bead of each round and don't be afraid to experiment with different types of accent beads (fig. 16). Don't limit yourself to the number of accent beads because several can be added in strands between columns. However, keep in mind that strands of between-column accent beads that are too long will cause the tube to collapse.

When working with large accent beads, add them every 2 or 3 rounds instead of every round. In the rounds where accent beads aren't added, follow the thread path of previous rounds to travel from one column to the next (fig. 17). This extra pass through the accent beads also helps secure them.

See Jean Power's **Twisty-Turny** necklace on page 114 for this technique and a clever way to add small sections of peyote stitch between columns.

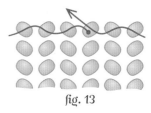

fig. 13

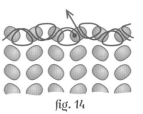

fig. 14

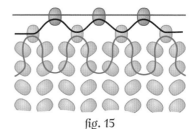

fig. 15

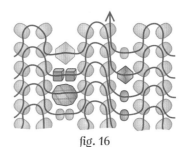

fig. 16

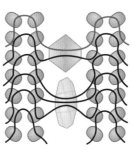

fig. 17

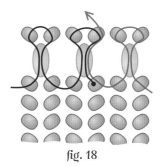

fig. 18

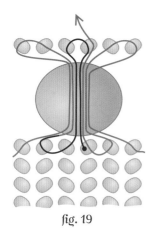

fig. 19

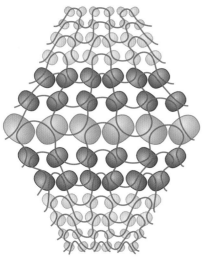

fig. 20

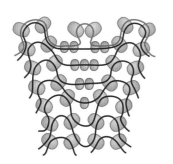

fig. 21

IN-COLUMN ACCENTS

Add accent beads within columns just as you did in the flat herringbone technique section (page 29) **(fig. 18, blue)**. Be sure to step up through the accent bead and the first bead of the first herringbone pair **(fig. 18, red)**.

In tubular herringbone stitch, all of the columns in a tube can share 1 accent bead. Work the first stitch as when adding any other accent bead **(fig. 19, blue)**. When working the stitches that follow, pass through the previous accent bead. At the end of the round, be sure to step up through the accent bead and the first bead of the first herringbone pair **(fig. 19, red)**. Keep in mind that the large accent bead must be able to accommodate several passes of thread. The order of the herringbone pairs at the top of the accent bead doesn't matter (unless you're working with different-colored columns and need to continue an established pattern). Just resume tubular herringbone as usual when working the next round.

If your accent bead has a large hole, the first pairs of herringbone beads added above the accent bead may slip down through this large hole. See the tips section on page 139 to learn how to alleviate this problem.

increases and decreases

Alter the shape and size of tubular herringbone with the use of accent beads as just described or try the following methods.

BEAD-SIZE CHANGE

Create wide and narrow sections in a rope by graduating from small to large beads and then back to small. For the most dramatic texture, work several rounds of size 15° seed beads, then a few rounds of 11°s, 8°s, and 6°s, and then reverse the order. Maintain tight tension when working the 8°s and 6°s; using doubled 6 lb braided beading thread will help. To add flexibility to the work, use slightly looser tension in the section of 15°s. Make sure you choose a thread color that blends well with your beads because some thread will show between the 8°s and 6°s **(fig. 20)**.

ADDING COLUMNS

To cause the beadwork to flare, work additional columns off of the increase beads placed between columns. To do so, add increase beads between columns as described above for several rounds to encourage the tube to expand. In 1 round, add 2 beads between 2 of the previously placed accent beads; the 2 beads just added become the base for a new herringbone column in the following rounds **(fig. 21)**. Use the thinnest beads in your bead tube for the initial increase pairs to keep the increase gradual.

DECREASING

To decrease the size of the tube, use fewer between-column accent beads. Or, play around with Vicki Star's decrease methods in the Flat Herringbone Stitch section on page 30. (Vicki's clever increase methods can be applied to tubular herringbone as well.)

Finishing Beaded Ropes

These techniques make it easy to give your beaded ropes a professional-looking finish:

CORE OF BEADS

To give your beaded rope more structure, add a strand of beads inside: Before stitching the end of the tube closed, use beading wire or durable braided beading thread to string enough same-colored beads to match the length of your rope. Make sure the beads are small enough to fit inside the rope's core.

To help guide the strand of beads through the center of the rope, use a piece of gauged scrap wire (20- or 22-gauge works well) that is longer than your tube as a makeshift needle: Use round-nose pliers to form a small simple or wrapped loop on one end of the gauged wire and tape the end of the loaded beading wire (or thread) to the other end of the gauged wire. Make sure the loop of the wire can pass through the circle formed by the rope's starting round(s). Pass the round end of the gauged wire through the tube, pushing the beadwork down over the strand of beads. Stitch through the final round of the rope with a ladder-stitched thread path to enclose the strand of beads **(fig. A)**.

CAPPED ENDS

To add a clean finish to the ends of your tubular-herringbone rope, form a small wrapped loop at the end of 4" (10 cm) of 20-, 22-, or 24-gauge wire. Insert the loop into the end of the rope and securely stitch the loop to the rope, passing back and forth between the sides of the rope. Secure the rope's thread and trim **(fig. B)**.

Use the wire end to string 1 bead cap or cone (wide end first) down over the end of the tube and form a wrapped loop **(fig. C)**. Attach your clasp or other design elements directly to this loop.

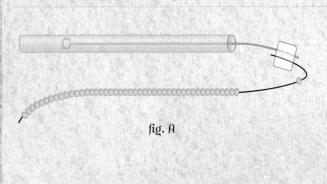

fig. A

fig. B

fig. C

Mix the playful texture of herringbone stitch with Indonesian striped glass beads in this one-size-fits-most bangle. Although the bangle seems to be made with strips of flat herringbone that hold the accent beads in place, it's actually worked quickly in the round. ● *by Melinda Barta*

tambourine bangles

TECHNIQUE
Tubular herringbone stitch

MATERIALS
11 g matte metallic bronze size 11° Japanese seed beads (A)

1 g matte silver sage permanent galvanized size 11° Japanese seed beads (B)

16 light blue with yellow and brown stripes 7–8×4mm Indonesian glass discs (C)

16 dark blue with white and brown stripes 7–8×4mm Indonesian glass discs (D)

Smoke 6 lb braided beading thread

TOOLS
Scissors

Size 10 and 12 beading needles

FINISHED SIZE
3" (inner diameter) (7.5 cm)

NOTES
Start with the size 10 needle and switch to the size 12 if you ever have trouble fitting the needle through beads.

The instructions given are for the bronze colorway. For information on the silver and purple variations, see page 89.

1 **Band.** Use tubular herringbone stitch to form the band:

ROUNDS 1 AND 2: Use 6' (183 cm) of thread to string {1B, 2A, and 1B} four times, leaving an 8" (20.5 cm) tail. Pass through the first 2 beads strung; don't tie a knot (**fig. 1**).

ROUND 3: String 2A and pass down through the next A previously strung, and then skip 2B and pass up through the following A; repeat three times to add a total of 8A (**fig. 2**). *Note:* Pull back on the tail thread as you work this and the following rounds to encourage the beads to stack. Step up for this and each subsequent round by passing through the first bead added in the current round. To keep the beadwork flexible, use relaxed thread tension.

ROUND 4: String 2A; pass down through the next bead of the previous round and up through the following bead of the previous round (**fig. 3, blue**). String 2A; pass down through the next 2A (A of Round 3 and A of Round 2), then pass up through the following 2A (A of Round 2 and A of Round 3). This begins to form the first opening in the side of the tube. Repeat from the beginning of this round to add a total of 8A and form the second opening (**fig. 3, red**). *Note:* The first 2 columns form one side of the band; the last 2 columns form the second side. Fold the tube to help establish these sides.

ROUND 5: String 2A; pass down through the next bead of the previous round and up through the following bead of the previous round (**fig. 4, blue**). String 2A; pass down through the next 3A (A of Round 4, A of Round 3, and A of Round 2), then pass up through the following 3A (A of Round 2, A of Round 3, and A of Round 4). Repeat from the beginning of this round to add a total of 8A (**fig. 4, red**).

ROUND 6: String 2A; pass down through the next bead of the previous round and up through the following bead of the previous round (**fig. 5, blue**). String 2A; pass down through the next 4A (A of Round 5, A of Round 4, A of Round 3, and A of Round 2), then pass up through the following 4A (A of Round 2, A of Round 3, A of Round 4, and A of Round 5). Repeat from the beginning of this round to add a total of 8A (**fig. 5, red**).

ROUND 7: String 2A; pass down through the next bead of the previous round and up through the following bead of the previous round (**fig. 6, blue**). String 2A; pass down

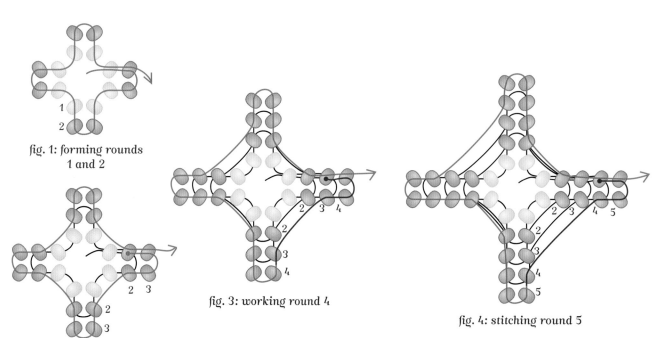

fig. 1: forming rounds 1 and 2

fig. 2: adding round 3

fig. 3: working round 4

fig. 4: stitching round 5

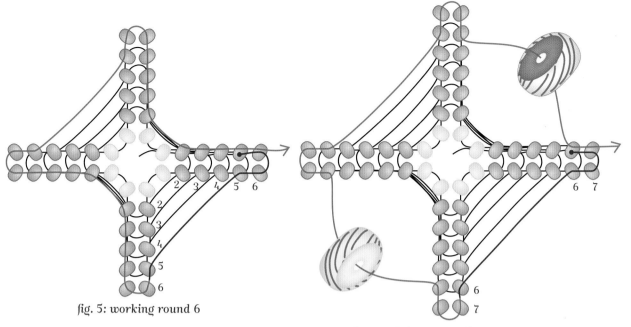

fig. 5: working round 6

fig. 6: stitching round 7 and adding discs

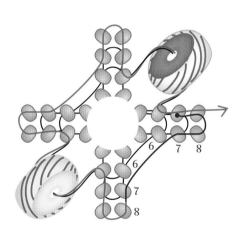

fig. 7: working round 8

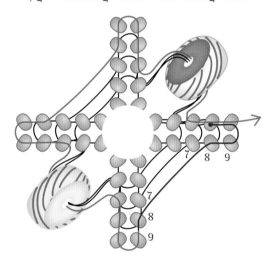

fig. 8: stitching round 9

through the next A of Round 6. String 1C; pass up through the following A of Round 6. *Note:* This places the C in the opening. Repeat from the beginning of this round, this time using 1D in place of the C (**fig. 6, red**).

ROUND 8: String 2A; pass down through the next bead of the previous round and up through the following bead of the

previous round (**fig. 7, blue**). String 2A; pass down through the next 2A (A of Round 7 and A of Round 6), then pass through the nearest disc and up through the following 2A (A of Round 6 and A of Round 7). Repeat from the beginning of this round to add a total of 8A (**fig. 7, red**).

ROUND 9: String 2A; pass down through the next bead of the

previous round and up through the following bead of the previous round (**fig. 8, blue**). String 2A; pass down through the next 2A (A of Round 8 and A of Round 7), then pass through the nearest disc and up through the following 2A (A of Round 7 and A of Round 8). Repeat from the beginning of this round to add a total of 8A (**fig. 8, red**).

ROUND 10: String 2A; pass down through the next bead of the previous round and up through the following bead of the previous round **(fig. 9, blue)**. String 2A; pass down through the next 3A (A of Round 9, A of Round 8, and A of Round 7), then pass through the nearest disc and up through the following 3A (A of Round 7, A of Round 8, and A of Round 9). Repeat from the beginning of this round to add a total of 8A **(fig. 9, red)**.

ROUND 11: String 2B; pass through the next bead of the previous round and up through the following bead of the previous round **(fig. 10, blue)**. String 2B; pass down through the next 4A (A of Round 10, A of Round 9, A of Round 8, and A of Round 7), then pass through the nearest disc and up through the following 4A (A of Round 7, A of Round 8, A of Round 9, and A of Round 10). Repeat from the beginning of this round to add a total of 8B **(fig. 10, red)**.

ROUND 12: String 2A and pass down through the next bead of the previous round and up through the following bead of the previous round; repeat three times to add a total of 8A and close the openings **(fig. 11)**. Repeat Rounds 3–12 fourteen times, or to the desired length, switching C and D every other round as desired to alternate the placement of the stripes along the edges of the bangle.

2 Join the ends. Repeat Rounds 3–10. To close the bangle, follow the thread path of Round 11, passing through the B of Round 1 instead of stringing new B beads **(fig. 12)**. Follow the thread path of Round 12, passing through Round 2 beads to reinforce the connection and close the ends. Secure the thread and trim. Add a needle to the tail thread and weave through beads of the connecting rounds to reinforce; secure the thread and trim.

TIPS

- Don't pull too tight in the round that adds the discs; otherwise, you might skew the direction of the herringbone beads along the edges.

- If you need to straighten the direction of any beads, weave down through the trouble bead(s), retracing previous thread paths. Just remember to skip from one side to the next by following the thread paths through the discs or the thread paths of Rounds 2 and/or 3.

- The pattern can be easily altered to incorporate almost any accent bead. Work more or fewer rounds in each repeat to accommodate different shapes, types, and sizes of beads.

- If adjusting the size of the bangle, be mindful of the C and D bead placements to continue the alternating pattern.

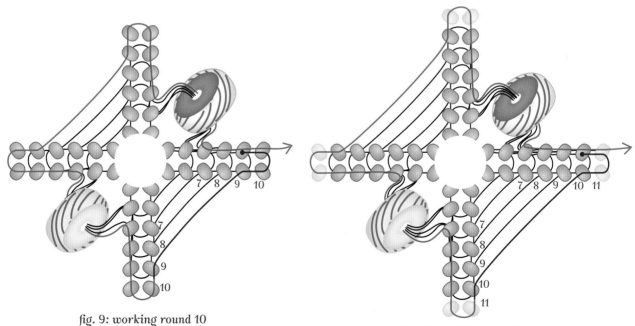

fig. 9: working round 10

fig. 10: stitching round 11

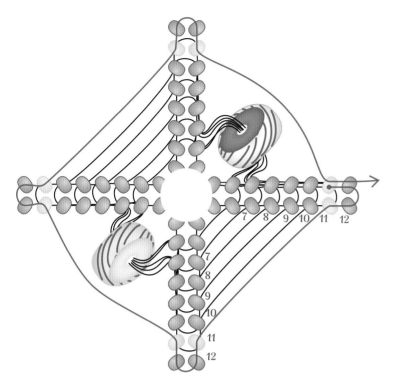

fig. 11: working round 12

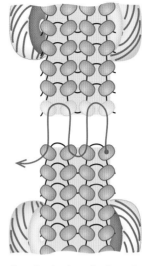

fig. 12: closing the bangle

DESIGN OPTIONS

BY MELINDA BARTA

Matte silver metallic beads are the perfect choice for these purple/white/red and red/white/black/blue striped discs because the mellow hue of silver does not overshadow the boldness of the stripes. The rounds of blue seed beads highlight the blue shades in the core of the red/white/black/blue discs.

Add more color to the mix by using different shades for the inside and outside edges of the bangle. Here, an earthy shade of light green is at the core with purple iris along the outer rim. White/brown/teal and red/white/purple glass discs add a funky, eclectic feel.

Named after the hip styles you'd find shopping the Hawthorne District of Portland, Oregon, this modish necklace is a mix of texture, color, and pattern. Top off the trendy look with a bit of dyed leather and wrapped wire. ● *by Melinda Barta*

hawthorne necklace

TECHNIQUES
Tubular herringbone stitch

Wireworking

MATERIALS
3 g light seafoam green size 13° Czech charlottes (A)

10 g turquoise-and-olive Picasso size 11° Czech seed beads (B)

4 g matte zinc size 11° metal seed beads (C)

0.5 g matte zinc size 8° metal seed beads (D)

2 green 9mm Lucite rounds

2 green 11mm Lucite rounds

1 green 13mm Lucite round

4 multicolored 18×22mm patterned lampwork ovals

1 oxidized sterling silver 13×20mm hook clasp

9" (23 cm) of sterling silver 22-gauge half-hard wire

12½" (31.5 cm) of dark blue 2mm round leather cord

Smoke 6 lb braided beading thread

TOOLS
Scissors

Size 10 and 12 beading needles

Sewing needle

Wire cutters

Chain- or flat-nose pliers

Round-nose pliers

FINISHED SIZE
18¾" (47.5 cm)

Note: The green 9–13mm Lucite rounds are core beads; feel free to substitute these with same-sized rounds of a different color and material because they won't show once beaded over. The Picasso-finish Czech size 11's used here run a bit thinner than your average Japanese size 11° seed beads. Make adjustments to the pattern, or to the size of the core beads, as needed, if substituting the Czech 11's for Japanese 11's. Start with the size 10 needle and switch to the size 12 if you ever have trouble fitting the needle through beads; the sewing needle is only used in Step 4.

1 Small beaded beads. Use
tubular herringbone stitch to cover the 9mm rounds with a layer of beadwork:

ROUNDS 1 AND 2: Use 6' (183 cm) of thread to string {4B and 1A} five times, leaving an 8" (20.5 cm) tail. Pass through the first 2 beads strung; don't tie a knot (**fig. 1**).

ROUND 3: String 2B and pass down through the next B, string 2A, skip 1B/A/1B of the starting circle, and pass up through the following B; repeat four times to add a total of 10B and 10A (**fig. 2**). *Note:* Pull back on the tail thread as you work this and the following rounds to encourage the beads to stack. Step up for this and each subsequent round by passing through the first bead added in the current round. To keep the beadwork flexible, use relaxed thread tension, but tight enough to encourage the beadwork to cup in the following rounds. Periodically press the 9mm round inside the beadwork to help shape it and to ensure the bead will fit inside the beadwork.

ROUND 4: String 2B and pass down through the next B of the previous round, then string 2A and pass up through the following B of the previous round; repeat four times to add a total of 10B and 10A (**fig. 3, blue**).

ROUND 5: String 2B and pass down through the next B of the previous round, then string 3A and pass up through the following B of the previous round; repeat four times to add a total of 10B and 15A (**fig. 3, red**).

ROUND 6: String 2B and pass down through the next B of the previous round, then string 1A, 1C, and 1A and pass up through the following B of the previous round; repeat four times to add a total of 10B, 10A, and 5C (**fig. 4**).

ROUND 7: Repeat Round 5. Insert the 9mm round. The beadwork will begin to decrease and pull up and around the core bead.

ROUNDS 8 AND 9: Repeat Round 4 twice. Keep the hole of the 9mm round aligned with the openings in the beadwork (see page 95 for tips).

CLOSE: Pass through the next B of Round 9. String 1A; pass through the following 2B of Round 9; repeat four times to add a total of 5A (**fig. 5**). Repeat the thread path to close the top of the beaded bead. Secure the thread and trim.

TAIL THREAD: Weave the tail through the B and A of Round 1 to close the starting end of the beaded bead. Secure the tail thread and trim. Set aside.

Repeat this entire step for a second small beaded bead.

2 Medium beaded beads.
Use tubular herringbone stitch to cover the 11mm rounds with a layer of beadwork:

ROUND 1: Use 6' (183 cm) of thread to string 10B, leaving an 8" (20.5 cm) tail. Pass through the first 2 beads strung; don't tie a knot (**fig. 6, blue**). *Note:* Pull back on the tail as you work the following rounds to encourage the beads to stack.

ROUND 2: String 2B and pass through the next 2B of Round 1; repeat four times to add a total of 10B (**fig. 6, red**). *Note:* Step up for this and each subsequent round by passing through the first bead added in the current round. To keep the beadwork flexible, use relaxed thread tension, but tight enough to encourage the beadwork to cup in the following rounds. Periodically press the 11mm round inside the beadwork to help shape it and to ensure the bead will fit inside the beadwork.

ROUND 3: String 2B and pass down through the next B of the previous round and then string 2A and pass up through the following B of the previous round; repeat four times to add a total of 10B and 10A (**fig. 7, orange**).

ROUND 4: String 2B and pass down through the next B of the previous round and then string 3A and pass up through the following B of the previous round; repeat four times to add a total of 10B and 15A (**fig. 7, purple**).

ROUND 5: String 2B and pass down through the next B of the previous round and then string

4A and pass up through the following B of the previous round; repeat four times to add a total of 10B and 20A **(fig. 7, green)**.

ROUND 6: String 2B and pass down through the next B of the previous round and then string 5A and pass up through the following B of the previous round; repeat four times to add a total of 10B and 25A **(fig. 7, blue)**.

ROUND 7: String 2B and pass down through the next B of the previous round and then string 2A, 1C, and 2A and pass up through the following B of the previous round; repeat four times to add a total of 10B, 20A, and 5C **(fig. 7, red)**.

ROUNDS 8–11: Insert the 11mm bead inside the beadwork and repeat Rounds 6–3 in that order.

CLOSE: Pass through all the beads of Round 11 **(fig. 8)**. Repeat the thread path to close the top of the beaded bead. Secure this thread and the tail thread and trim. Set aside.

Repeat this entire step for a second medium beaded bead.

3 Large beaded bead. Use tubular herringbone stitch to cover the 13mm round with a layer of beadwork:

ROUNDS 1–6: Repeat Step 2, Rounds 1–6 **(fig. 9, black)**.

ROUND 7: String 2B and pass down through the next B of the previous round and then string 6A and pass up through the following B of the previous round; repeat four times to add a total of 10B and 30A **(fig. 9, blue)**.

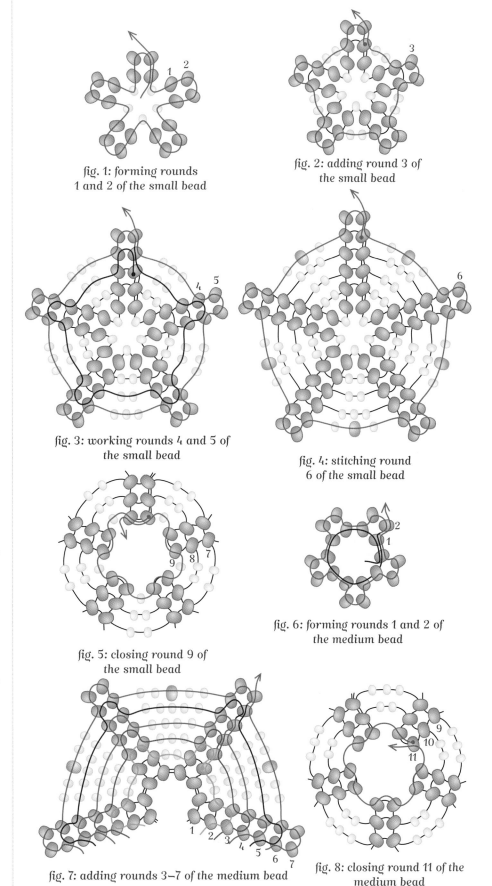

fig. 1: forming rounds 1 and 2 of the small bead

fig. 2: adding round 3 of the small bead

fig. 3: working rounds 4 and 5 of the small bead

fig. 4: stitching round 6 of the small bead

fig. 5: closing round 9 of the small bead

fig. 6: forming rounds 1 and 2 of the medium bead

fig. 7: adding rounds 3–7 of the medium bead

fig. 8: closing round 11 of the medium bead

ROUND 8: String 2B and pass down through the next B of the previous round and then string 3A, 1C, and 3A and pass up through the following B of the previous round; repeat four times to add a total of 10B, 30A, and 5C **(fig. 9, red)**.

ROUNDS 9–13: Insert the 13mm bead inside the beadwork and repeat Rounds 7–3 in that order.

CLOSE: Repeat Step 2, Close (refer to **fig. 8**), passing through all the beads of Round 13. Set aside.

4 **Straps.** Use two-drop tubular herringbone stitch to bead ropes and finish with leather cord and wire:

ROUNDS 1 AND 2: Use 6' (183 cm) of thread to string {4B and 1C} three times, leaving an

8" (20.5 cm) tail. Pass through the first 2 beads strung; don't tie a knot **(fig. 10)**. *Note:* Pull back on the tail as you work the following rounds to encourage the beads to stack.

ROUND 3: String 2B and pass down through the next 2B/C/2B of the starting circle; repeat twice to add a total of 6B **(fig. 11, blue)**. Step up by passing through the first bead added in this round.

ROUND 4: String 4B and pass down through the next B of the previous round and then string 1C and pass up through the following B of the previous round; repeat twice to add a total of 12B and 3C **(fig. 11, red)**. *Note:* Step up for this and each subsequent round by

passing through the first *2 beads* added in the current round.

ROUNDS 5 AND ON: Repeat Round 4 until the rope measures 4⅛" (10.3 cm) or the desired length. Don't trim the thread.

CORD, LOOP 1: Pass one end of one 6¼" (16 cm) piece of cord down through the center of the rope to exit Rounds 1 and 2. Tie a knot at the end of 12" (30.5 cm) of new thread and add the sewing needle to the end. Working on the end of the cord nearest the final round of the rope, fold down the final ½" (1.3 cm) of the cord onto itself. Sew down the end of the cord to form a ¼" (6 mm) loop, using pliers, if needed, to push and pull the needle through the cord **(fig. 12)**. Tie several half-hitch

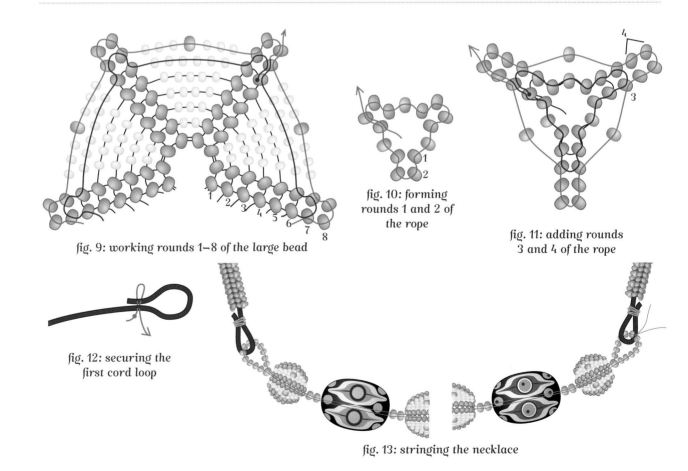

fig. 9: working rounds 1–8 of the large bead

fig. 10: forming rounds 1 and 2 of the rope

fig. 11: adding rounds 3 and 4 of the rope

fig. 12: securing the first cord loop

fig. 13: stringing the necklace

knots before trimming the thread. Push the rope down the cord to meet the end of the loop.

CLOSE: Pass the needle exiting the final round of the rope through the next B of the final round. String 1C; pass through the next 2B of the final round; repeat twice to add a total of 3C. Repeat the thread path to close the top of the rope. Secure the thread and trim.

CORD, LOOP 2: Fold the other end of the cord onto itself to form a second ¼" (6 mm) loop. Trim the end. Sew down as for Loop 1. Add a needle to the tail thread and pass through the 3C and 6B of Round 1 several times to close the end of the rope. Secure the thread and trim.

WIRE: Use round-nose pliers to make a small half-loop (about ⅛" [3 mm]) at one end of one 4½" (11.5 cm) piece of wire. Catch the half-loop over one of the cords over the stitches that hold the loop together. Tightly wrap

the wire seven or eight times around the cords, covering the stitches. Trim the wire and tuck the tip between wraps, using pliers, if needed, to help shape the wire. Repeat this section to cover the base of the other loop with wire.

Repeat this entire step for a second strap, enclosing the clasp in one of the loops.

5 Assembly: Add the size 10 beading needle to the center of 6' (183 cm) of thread and bring the ends together to form a 3' (91.5 cm) doubled thread. Leaving an 8" (20.5 cm) tail, string 6C, 1D, 1 small beaded bead, 2D, and 1 oval. *Note:* If the D beads slip inside the holes in your lampwork oval, string as many as needed to ensure that 2 show between each beaded bead and oval. String 2D, 1 medium beaded bead, 2D, 1 oval, 2D, the large beaded bead, 2D, 1 oval, 2D, 1 medium beaded bead, 2D, 1 oval, 2D, 1 small beaded bead, 1D, 6C, the loop that's opposite the

clasp on one strap, and 6C. Pass back through all of the beads to exit the first D strung. String 6C, pass through 1 loop of the remaining strap, snug the beads, and tie the tail and working threads together with a tight overhand knot **(fig. 13)**. Repeat the entire thread path. Secure the threads and trim.

TIPS

- All Czech seed beads vary slightly in size, so keep in mind you may need to adjust the number of A added between the columns of B to keep the work flat. If adjusting the size of the core bead, or if using an oval bead, you'll need to change the number of rounds worked.

- If desired, use a small piece of wire to keep the hole of the core bead aligned with the openings in the beaded cover. If you lose the place of the center hole, use a needle to push and rotate the core bead until the holes are aligned.

How to Oxidize Silver

Oxidize the sterling silver wire before you wrap the cords for a modern and professional look. Use this super-easy and nontoxic method:

1: Hard-boil an egg.

2: While the egg is still warm, smash it in an airtight plastic container or a zip-close plastic bag and lay the wire on top of the egg.

3: Close the lid/bag and let sit for 30–60 minutes, or until the wire is as dark as you like. Remember you can always lighten the wire later.

4: Remove the wire and wash it in warm soapy water.

5: Wrap the cords as in Step 4 for the necklace and use a silver polishing cloth to remove the oxidation on the outside surface of the wire.

Six decorative beaded collars, sprinkled with twinkling crystal bicones, gracefully orbit three beaded ropes made of odd-count tubular herringbone stitch. For the closure, stitch two more collars to elegantly conceal the magnetic clasps at the rope ends. ● *by Melinda Barta*

constellations necklace

TECHNIQUES
Tubular herringbone stitch

Ladder stitch

Picot

MATERIALS
0.5 g silver gray opaque gold luster size 15° Japanese seed beads (A)

28 g nickel silver electroplate size 11° Japanese seed beads (B)

7 g smoked gray opaque gold luster size 11° Japanese seed beads (C)

2 g matte metallic dark brown size 11° Japanese seed beads (D)

1 g ice blue bronze gold luster size 11° Japanese seed beads (E)

4 g metallic plum copper size 11° Japanese seed beads (F)

1 g metallic red copper size 11° Japanese seed beads (G)

155 silver shade 2.5mm crystal bicones

2 gunmetal 5×7mm round magnetic clasp sets

Smoke 6 lb braided beading thread

TOOLS
Scissors

Size 10 and 12 beading needles

FINISHED SIZE
17¾" (45 cm) (shortest strand)

NOTE
Start with the size 10 needle and switch to the size 12 if you ever have trouble fitting the needle through beads.

1 Ropes. Make 3 triangular ropes using a variation of tubular herringbone stitch:

Note: Use a "bead soup" mix of B, C, D, and E seed beads and bicones for the ropes, using more B than any other color (see tip on page 100). The quantity of bicones called for in the materials list assumes 1 bicone is placed every ¾" to 1" (2 to 2.5 cm). Set aside 48 bicones to use for the collars.

fig. 1: forming round 1

fig. 2: working round 2

fig. 3: flattened side view of stitching round 2

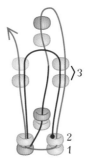

fig. 4: working round 3

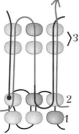

fig. 5: flattened side view of stitching round 3

fig. 6: closing gaps in the rope by stitching down through several rounds

ROPE ROUND 1: Use 6' (183 cm) of thread to ladder-stitch a strip 1 bead high and 3 beads long, leaving a 10" (25.5 cm) tail **(fig. 1, blue)**. Stitch the first and last beads together to form a ring **(fig. 1, red)**.

ROPE ROUND 2: String 2 beads; pass down through the next bead of Rope Round 1 and up through the following bead of Rope Round 1 **(fig. 2, blue; flattened side view in fig. 3, blue)**. String 1 bead; pass down through the first bead of this round and the next bead of Rope Round 1, then pass up through the following bead of Rope Round 1 and the second bead added in this round **(fig. 2, red; flattened side view in fig. 3, red)**.

ROPE ROUND 3: String 4 beads; pass down through the next bead of the previous round and up through the following bead of the previous round **(fig. 4, blue; flattened side view in fig. 5, blue)**. String 2 beads; pass down through the first 2 beads of this round and the next bead of the previous round, then pass up through the following bead of the previous round and the fourth and third beads added in this round **(fig. 4, red; flattened side view in fig. 5, red)**.

ROPE ROUNDS 4 AND ON: Repeat Rope Round 3 until the rope measures 17" (43 cm), mixing the beads as desired.

Note: If any gaps in the rope form due to differences in tension or if you need to straighten out a bicone, you can weave down through several beads in a column instead of passing down just through the previous round **(fig. 6)**. Just be sure to correctly weave

up through the next column to properly set up for the next round.

Repeat this entire step until the second rope measures 18" (45.5 cm). Repeat again for a 19" (48.5 cm) rope. Set the 3 ropes aside.

2 Collars. Use tubular herringbone stitch to form decorative collars for the ropes:

COLLAR ROUNDS 1 AND 2: Use 4' (122 cm) of thread to string {4F and 1G} six times for a total of 24F and 6G; pass through the first 2F **(fig. 7)**.

COLLAR ROUND 3: String 2F, pass down through the next F of Collar Round 2, string 1A, then skip the next 3 beads of Collar Round 1 and pass up through the following F; repeat twice to add a total of 6F and 3A **(fig. 8, blue)**. String 2F, pass down through the next F of Collar Round 2, string 1 bicone, then skip the next 3 beads of Collar Round 1 and pass up through the following F; repeat twice to add 6 more F and 3 bicones **(fig. 8, red)**.

Note: Step up for this and each subsequent round by passing through the first bead added in the current round. Work with relaxed tension to avoid cutting your thread on the crystals. The reinforcement round after Round 5 will help pull the collar into a perfect cylinder.

COLLAR ROUND 4: String 2F, pass down through the next F of Collar Round 3, string 1A, and pass up through the following F of Collar Round 3; repeat twice to add a total of 6F and 3A **(fig. 9, blue)**. String 2F, pass down through the next 2F (F of Collar Round 3 and F of Collar

Round 2), the nearest bicone, and up through the following 2F (F of Collar Round 2 and F of Collar Round 3); repeat twice to add 6 more F (**fig. 9, red**).

COLLAR ROUND 5: String 1F, 1G, and 1F, pass down through the next F of Collar Round 4 to form a picot, string 1A, and pass up through the following F of Collar Round 4; repeat twice to add a total of 6F, 3G, and 3A (**fig. 10, blue**). String 1F, 1G, and 1F, pass down through the next F of Collar Round 4 to form a picot, string 1 bicone, and pass up through the following F of Collar Round 4; repeat twice to add 6 more F, 3 more G, and 3 bicones (**fig. 10, red**). Secure the thread and trim.

COLLAR REINFORCEMENT: Use the tail thread and tight tension to weave up and down through all columns and end G beads (**fig. 11**). This will pull the collar into a perfect cylinder in case you had any distortion. If any round feels loose, retrace the thread path of that round. It's also a good idea to retrace Rounds 3 and 5 to reinforce the bicones. Secure the thread and trim. Set aside.

Repeat this entire step seven times for a total of 8 collars.

3 Assembly. Join the ropes, add the clasps, and stitch the collars in place:

ROPE ENDS: Hold the ropes so each triangular side lies against the next with the bottom of Round 1 aligned and the 18" (45.5 cm) rope in the middle (**fig. 12;** view of rope ends). Use a tail thread to stitch the ends together, passing through the beads of Round 1 with a ladder-stitch thread path. Secure this thread and trim; leave the remaining tails intact. Making sure the ropes aren't twisted, repeat this section using the working threads of the ropes and passing through the final rounds.

CLASPS: Weave 1 tail thread through beads to exit Round 1 of the 17" (43 cm) rope. String one half of 1 clasp, pass down through the next bead of Rope Round 1, and pass up through the following bead (**fig. 13, blue**). Pass through the clasp, pass down through the next bead of Rope Round 1, and pass up through the following bead (**fig. 13, red**). Repeat the thread path several times to secure the clasp, stitching down through more than just the end round for extra security. Secure the thread and trim.

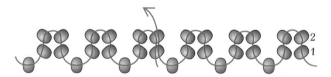

fig. 7: forming collar rounds 1 and 2

fig. 8: stitching collar round 3

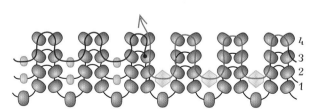

fig. 9: working collar round 4

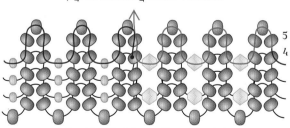

fig. 10: stitching collar round 5

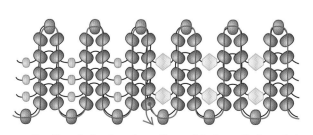

fig. 11: reinforcing the collar with the tail thread

fig. 12: aligning the rope ends

fig. 13: attaching one half of 1 clasp

99

Weave the remaining tail thread through beads to exit Round 1 of the 19" (48.5 cm) rope and attach one half of the other clasp, making sure this clasp half is the same polarity as the one just added so the clasps don't snap together. Secure the thread and trim.

Repeat this entire section to attach clasps to the other ends of the ropes, using the remaining working and tail threads. Secure the threads and trim.

ROPE JOINS: Close the clasps and spread the necklace out on your work surface, with the shortest rope on the inside. Add a needle to 12" (30.5 cm) of new thread and pass through all 3 ropes between beads in the place where you want the first collar below the clasp, leaving a 5" tail (12.5 cm) (see **fig. 14** for placement; measurements are of the inner edge of the shortest rope segments between joins). Pass through 2 beads of the outside edge of the outside rope and back through the ropes again

(fig. 15). Before securing the thread, try the necklace on to see if you're happy with the drape around your neck. Remove the thread and adjust if needed. If you're happy with the placement, repeat the thread path several times. Secure the working and tail threads; trim only the tail thread. Repeat this entire section seven times to secure a new thread to each position marked in **fig. 14**. *Note:* The ropes in the center swag are meant to separate slightly, so work the joins from the clasps going forward, leaving any excess rope for the center.

ATTACH COLLARS: Use the left end of the ropes to string 1 collar, passing through the end of the collar with Rounds 1 and 2 first. Flatten the collar so the 6 bicones are on top. Slide it down over the bottom left join and use the join's thread to stitch the collar in place over the join. Repeat twice on the left side of the necklace, covering the other two joins, then stitch the final collar over the ends of

the ropes, allowing it to slightly overhang the rope ends to cover the clasp. *Note:* Make sure all of the bicones on the collars are faceup.

Use the right end of the ropes to repeat this section on the three right joins on the necklace, again being sure to pass through the ends of the collars with Rounds 1 and 2 first. Add the final collar over the right end of the ropes and clasp, but this time pass through the end of the collar with Round 5 first. *Note:* The end collars will interlock to cover the clasps when the necklace is closed.

TIPS

- Instead of trying on the necklace when placing the joins, drape the ropes over a neck form if you have one. The goal is to make sure the ropes smoothly follow the curve of your neck.

- If you opt to go without the stitched clasp cover and magnets, a sliding tube clasp makes a good substitute.

- When making "bead soup" in Step 1, mix the beads in batches. This way if you change your mind on rope length, you won't have to sort all of the beads later if you mix too much. Also, the weight of seed beads can vary greatly depending on the coating/finished surface of the beads you choose. That said, the number of grams called for in the materials list is a starting point, not necessarily the amount you should mix into your soup.

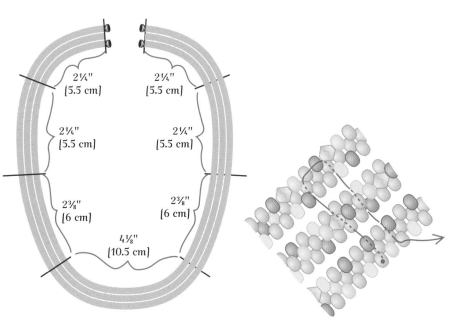

fig. 14: blue lines mark the placement of the rope joins

2¼" [5.5 cm]

2¼" [5.5 cm]

2¼" [5.5 cm]

2¼" [5.5 cm]

2⅜" [6 cm]

2⅜" [6 cm]

4⅛" [10.5 cm]

fig. 15: joining the ropes

DESIGN OPTION

Roped In Necklace

BY MELINDA BARTA

In this classy variation of my Constellations Necklace (page 96), three different lengths of beautifully draping beaded rope (beaded by Katie Nelson) are joined with a knot. A pair of beaded collars conceals the clasps.

MATERIALS

0.5 g metallic cabernet iris size 15° Japanese seed beads

40 g total bronze/gold mix of size 11° Japanese seed beads including metallic light bronze, metallic dark bronze, and 24k gold electroplate

6 g metallic plum hematite size 11° Japanese seed beads

0.5 g metallic cabernet iris size 11° Japanese seed beads

4 g metallic light bronze size 11° Japanese cylinder beads

110 dark blue 2mm pearls

12 bronze 3mm pressed-glass rounds

2 brass 5×7mm round magnetic clasp sets

Smoke 6 lb braided beading thread

TOOLS

Scissors

Size 12 beading needles

FINISHED SIZE

23½" (59.5 cm) (shortest strand)

1 ROPES. Repeat Step 1 for the Constellations Necklace (page 96) to make one 32" (81.5 cm) rope, one 29½" (75 cm) rope, and one 27" (68.5 cm) rope, using "bead soup" made of cylinder beads, pearls, metallic plum hematite size 11°s, and the gold/bronze mix. Set aside.

2 COLLARS. Repeat Step 2 for the Constellations Necklace using metallic plum hematite in place of F for the herringbone columns, metallic cabernet iris size 11°s at the tip of each column, metallic cabernet iris size 15°s in place of A, and the 3mm rounds in place of bicones. Set aside.

Repeat this entire step for a second collar.

3 ASSEMBLY. Repeat Step 3, Rope Ends, for the Constellations Necklace to join the ends of the ropes. To give the ropes an overlapping look, join the shortest rope between the 2 longest ropes. Attach the clasps as in Step 3. Attach the collars over the ends of the ropes to conceal the clasps as in Step 3.

4 KNOT. Use all 3 ropes to tie an overhand knot on the right side of the necklace, about 7" (18 cm) down from the clasp. Gently push and pull the strands until the knot is smooth and the strands above the knot lie flat. If desired, start 12" (30.5 cm) of new thread in one of the ropes and sew the strands together in the center of the knot to secure it. Secure the thread and trim.

twists and spirals

Play around with thread paths, step-ups, and bead size and witness your herringbone tubes and ropes magically transform into twists and spirals. To understand the subtle difference, think of the decorative lines on a barber shop's pole or the Cape Hatteras Lighthouse when imagining a twist. For a spiral, think of a rotini noodle or an auger. Plus, you can apply some of these methods to circular herringbone stitch to add flair to your designs.

Jill Wiseman's **Rolling in the Deep** bracelet features a subtly striped spiral herringbone rope made of size 15°, 11°, and 8° seed beads; a tubular herringbone toggle bar; and sparkly flat herringbone crystal sliders. Best of all, the sliders are removable and interchangeable, giving you a design with mileage.

In **Twisty-Turny**, Jean Power shows how adding a simple spiral thread path and between-column accent beads takes a basic tubular rope far beyond the ordinary. Plus, the design is as versatile as it gets—wear it as a long necklace, a double-wrap necklace, or a playful wrapped bracelet.

A true display of the beauty and versatility of herringbone stitch, Leslie Frazier's **Buena Vista** necklace features asymmetrical flat herringbone straps made with triangle beads, plus gorgeous flowers created with an amazing spiral variation of circular herringbone.

TECHNIQUES

twisted tubular herringbone

Although there are countless ways to set tubular herringbone into a spin, this section explains the most common. With all of these variations, expect to work 1" to 2" (2.5 to 5 cm) of rope before the twist pattern appears. Choose the variation to suit your design or choose the one that best suits your ease of stitching based on thread tension, angle of beads, size of beads, handedness, etc. (Sometimes it's easier to go down 2 beads and up 1 bead than down 1 bead and up 2 beads—or vice versa.) The instructions below assume you stitch your tubes clockwise (when looking down on the current round); if you stitch counterclockwise, expect your work to twist in the opposite direction.

DOWN ONE, UP TWO

This variation will cause the beadwork to twist to the left. Work 3 rounds of tubular herringbone as usual. Starting in Round 4, change your thread path to set the twist: String 2 beads and pass down through the next bead in the current column, then pass up through the top 2 beads of the next column (**fig. 1, green**). Continue working the round, adding 2 beads in each stitch, and following this *down 1, up 2* pattern (**fig. 1, blue**). For the final stitch, be sure to step up through the first bead added, using a *down 1, up 3* pattern to complete the round (**fig. 1, red**).

DOWN TWO, UP ONE

By reversing the thread pattern for the *down 1, up 2* variation, the tube will twist to the right instead of the left. When beading around, think *down 2, up 1* (**fig. 2, blue**). For the final stitch, think *down 2, up 2* (**fig. 2, red**).

DOWN THREE, UP ONE

For a more dramatic twist, begin by working 4 rounds of regular tubular herringbone. Follow

down 1, up 2

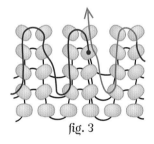

down 3, up 1

fig. 1

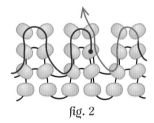

fig. 3

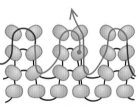

fig. 2

a *down 3, up 1* thread path until you reach the final stitch (**fig. 3, blue**). For the final stitch, work *down 3, up 2* to include the step-up (**fig. 3, red**). This also works following a *down 1, up 3* pattern to twist the work in the other direction. If you'd like to start

twisting before working 4 full rounds of regular tubular herringbone, follow a *down 2, up 1* thread path while working Round 3—you now have enough beads to begin the *down 3, up 1* pattern in Round 4.

STEP-UP CHANGE

Instead of changing the thread pattern with each stitch, just change the final stitch's step-up. In this example, work the round in regular tubular herringbone until you reach the final stitch (**fig. 4, blue**). For the final stitch (and step-up), follow a *down 1, up 3* pattern (**fig. 4, red**). Following a *down 1, up 4* thread path for the step-up will produce a more dramatic twist, but be sure to use tight thread tension to avoid exposed thread.

NO STEP-UP

For a subtle twist that's a breeze to stitch—and without any involved thread patterns to remember—skip the step-up altogether! Work the round in regular tubular herringbone (**fig. 5, blue**) *and* the final stitch in the same *down 1, up 1* manner (**fig. 5, red**).

BEAD-SIZE AND -TYPE CHANGE FOR TWISTS

Play around with different-sized beads and bead types in your twisted ropes to form interesting patterns, textures, and degrees of twist.

In this example, worked in the *down 1, up 2* variation, each herringbone stitch consists of 1 size 11° cylinder bead and 1 size 15° seed bead (**fig. 6, blue**). *Note:* Stringing the size 11° before the size 15° works best because the column of 11°s will begin to pull down over the 15°s, accentuating the twist. The top round is beginning to introduce contrasting size 8° beads in place of the size 11° cylinder beads (**fig. 6, red**); by doing this every other round, the size 8°s will begin to form vertical lines that spiral up the rope. Substitute the size 8°s with different accent beads, such as small drops, for an array of effects. And you don't have

to substitute each size 11° cylinder bead in the round; for fewer stripes, substitute only a couple.

Adding contrasting size 8° beads in every round in this example will create a more dramatic twist. However, when the larger beads begin to stack on top of each other, you'll start to notice exposed threads between beads. You can reduce the amount of exposed thread by using tighter tension, but, in my experience with this variation, this just leads to broken threads.

For a rope with a ribbed texture, alternate 1 size 11° and 1 size 8° seed bead (or 2 other bead choices similar in size) in your starting ring of ladder stitch. In each of the following stitches, the first bead of the herringbone pair should match the bead last exited; the second bead of the herringbone pair needs to match the bead you're about to pass down through.

spiral herringbone

Very similar in technique to twisted tubular herringbone, these variations give ropes an added sense of dimension—not only do the vertical patterns twist, but also the rope as a whole begins to spiral. The instructions below assume you stitch your tubes clockwise (when looking down on the current round); if you stitch counterclockwise, expect your work to twist in the opposite direction.

BEAD-SIZE CHANGE FOR SPIRALS

Mixing small and large beads in a rope can accentuate the twist. If using size 15° and 8° seed beads in a design, add pairs of 11°s in between to help make the size difference between the largest and smallest beads more gradual (**fig. 7**). Note that a change in bead size isn't

enough to complete the twist. The bead-size change will only encourage the work to curve. You'll also need to work a *down 1, up 2* (or other) thread pattern. See Jill Wiseman's take on this variation in her Rolling In the Deep bracelet (page 108).

DOUBLE HELIX SPIRAL

This great variation of tubular herringbone forms 2 flat bands edged by larger beads, resulting in a double helix. Plus, after Round 2, there's no step-up required! Follow this example, which spirals to the right, then play around with your own variations:

ROUND 1: Ladder-stitch a strip 6 seed beads wide and 1 bead tall for Round 1 in this order: 2 size 11°s, 1 size 8°, 2 size 11°s, and 1 size 8°. Join the first and last beads to form a ring. Weave through beads to exit up through 1 size 11°, just to the right of 1 size 8°.

ROUND 2: String 1 size 11° and 1 size 8°; pass down through the next bead of Round 1 and up through the following bead. String 2 size 11°s; pass down through the next bead of Round 1 and up through the following bead. String 1 size 8° and 1 size 11°; pass down through the next bead of Round 1 and up through the following bead and step up through the first bead added in this round (**fig. 8, blue**).

ROUNDS 3 AND ON: Stitch the following in regular (with a down 1, up 1 pattern) tubular herringbone stitch: Work 1 stitch with 1 size 11° and 1 size 8°. Work 1 stitch with 2 size 11°s. For the final stitch, string 1 size 8° and 1 size 11° but don't step up; instead, only pass up through the first bead of this round (**fig. 8, red**). Repeat this entire round when working all following rounds. After you skip the first step-up in Round 3, the *down 1, up 1* pattern will come naturally. As you work, flatten the sides of the rope, about ¾" (2 cm) down from the current round, so size 8°s border each edge. If you flatten the beadwork after each round, it may be difficult to tighten the thread that helps angle the beads for the spiral.

SPIRALING NARROW BAND

Here's an easy way to make a narrow band—which is great for clasp loops, straps, and more—spiral to the left. Although it is technically a variation of square stitch, you may hear other designers call the technique used here 2-bead or single-column herringbone. After working 3 rows, orient the beadwork with the thread exiting the top left bead. *Note:* It's helpful to use 2 different colors in each row to help you keep track of the left and right beads. String 2 beads; pass down through the next bead of the previous row on the right side of the band. Then pass up through the top 2 beads on the left side of the band and the first bead just added (**fig. 9, blue**). Continue in this *down 1, up 3* pattern for the length of the band (**fig. 9, red**).

BETWEEN-COLUMN ACCENT BEADS

In Jean Power's Twisty-Turny necklace (page 114), pairing one line of between-column accent beads, in addition to an alternate thread path, creates a fun and decorative spiraling rope.

rope with drops

double helix spiral

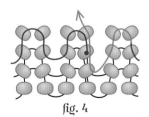

fig. 4

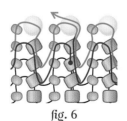

fig. 6

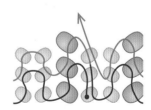

fig. 8

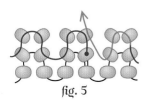

fig. 5

fig. 7

fig. 9

TIPS

- When first learning twists and spirals, work every other round in a different color to keep track of where to step up for the next round. Or, choose a different color for each column.

- If you work with tight tension and find it difficult to step up through several beads at once, pinch just the step-up beads and gently pull them away from the surrounding beadwork. This will give you just enough space for your needle to fit.

- Count out the beads for each round. When you run out, it's time to step up.

- Make up a mantra. For example, to me, "small, big, down, up, small, small, down, up, big, small, down, up" translated to the bead sizes and thread paths in the double helix spiral. Use whatever works for you!

- If you miss the step-up at the end of the round, just keep working. Your rope might end up with a little more twist/spiral than those described here, but simply continue stitching in the established pattern and see what evolves.

Spiral Circular Herringbone

Leslie Frazier has found amazing ways to incorporate spiraling techniques into her circular herringbone designs. See her Buena Vista necklace (page 120) to learn how to make her signature spiraling flowers.

Learn the basics of the technique by following this sample, then play around with your own variations:

ROUND 1: Work a loose ladder-stitched strip 10 size 11° Japanese seed beads long and 1 bead high. Square-stitch the first and last beads together to form a ring.

ROUND 2: String 3 size 11° cylinder beads and 1 size 11° Japanese seed bead, then pass down through the next bead of Round 1 and up through the following bead; repeat four times to add a total of 15 cylinder beads and 5 seed beads. Step up through the first 3 size 11°s added in this round **(fig. A, green)**. *Note:* The 3 cylinder beads form the right side of each column while 1 seed bead

forms the left side of each column; this difference in size and bead count begins forming the spiral.

ROUND 3: String 1 cylinder bead and 1 seed bead, then pass through the next seed bead of the previous round and up through the top 3 cylinder beads of the following column; repeat this entire *down 1, up 3* sequence four times to add a total of 5 cylinder beads and 5 seed beads. In the final stitch, think *down 1, up 4* to step up through the first bead of this round **(fig. A, blue)**. See page 125 to work without a step-up at the end of the round.

ROUND 4: String 1 cylinder bead and 1 seed bead; pass down through the next seed bead of the previous round. String 1 seed bead; pass up through the top 3 cylinder beads of the next column. *Note:* The seed bead between the herringbone columns just added is an increase bead; add as many or as few as

desired to shape the work. Repeat this entire *down 1, up 3* (or think of it as down 1, add 1, up 3 including the increase bead) sequence four times to add a total of 5 cylinder beads and 10 seed beads. Use a *down 1, up 4* pattern as at the end of Round 3 for the step-up **(fig. A, red)**.

ROUNDS 5 AND ON: To keep the work flat, continue to add more or larger accent beads between columns. Or, work sections of peyote stitch as in the Buena Vista necklace.

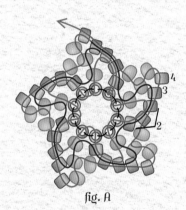

fig. A

Jazz up a spiral herringbone bracelet with clever interchangeable rings that slide back and forth along the rope. A tubular peyote-stitch toggle ring with a tubular herringbone toggle completes the bracelet.
● *by Jill Wiseman*

rolling in the deep

TECHNIQUES
Ladder stitch

Flat, tubular, and spiral tubular herringbone stitch

Square stitch

Tubular peyote stitch

Zipping

Picot

Fringe

MATERIALS
2.5 g silver-lined clear size 15° seed beads (A)

10 g matte metallic dark blue iris size 11° seed beads (B)

15 g metallic blue–lined clear size 8° seed beads (C)

32 jet 2XAB 3mm crystal bicones (D)

Smoke 6 lb braided beading thread

2 medium-sized paper clips

Clear tape

TOOLS
Scissors

Size 10 beading needles

Memory wire cutters

FINISHED SIZE
8" (20.5 cm)

NOTE
The instructions given are for the blue colorway. For information on the gold variation, see page 113.

1 Rope. Use ladder and spiral tubular herringbone stitches to form the bracelet's rope:

ROUND 1: Use 6' (183 cm) of thread to ladder-stitch a strip 1 bead high and 8 beads long in this order: 2B, 2C, 2B, and 2A, leaving a 2' (61 cm) tail (**fig. 1, purple**). Ladder-stitch the first and last beads together to form a ring (**fig. 1, red**). *Note:* Make sure you're exiting up through the first B and the second B is to the left of it. If the second B is not to the left of the first B, undo the ladder-stitch join and restitch, making sure you orient the strip so you're holding the 2A to the right of the first pair of 2B as in **fig. 1**.

ROUND 2: String 2B; pass down through the next B of Round 1 and up through the nearest C of Round 1. String 2C; pass down through the next C of Round 1 and up through the nearest B of Round 1. String 2B; pass down through the next B of Round 1 and up through the nearest A of Round 1. String 2A; pass down through the next A of Round 1 and up through the nearest B of Round 1 (**fig. 2, purple**). *Note:* Step up for this and each subsequent round by passing through the first bead added in the current round.

ROUND 3: Work tubular herringbone stitch with 2 beads in each stitch in this order: 2B, 2C, 2B, and 2A (**fig. 2, red**). *Note:* The beads added here should match the beads of the column below, continuing in the established pattern.

ROUND 4: String 2B; pass down through the next 2B (B beads of the 2 previous rounds) and up through the following top C of the previous round (**fig. 3, purple**). String 2C; pass down through the next 2C (C beads of the 2 previous rounds) and up through the following top B of the previous round (**fig. 3, green**). String 2B; pass down through the next 2B (B beads of the 2 previous rounds) and up through the following top A of the previous round (**fig. 3, blue**). String 2A; pass down through the next 2A (A beads of the 2 previous rounds) and up through the following 2B (the top B of the previous round and the first B added in the current round). *Note:* The *down 2, up 1* pattern establishes the spiral; think *down 2, up 2* for the fourth stitch because of the step-up (**fig. 3, red**).

ROUNDS 5–118: Repeat Round 4 one hundred fourteen times or to the desired length minus 1¾" (4.5 cm) for the final rounds and clasp. Be sure to try the rope on your wrist because extra length is required because of the spiral (see tip on page 112 for more sizing information).

FINAL ROUNDS: Repeat Round 3 four times. Join the beads of the last round using a ladder-stitch thread path. Secure the thread and trim. Set aside.

2 Clasp ring. Use tubular peyote stitch to form a clasp ring by stitching two sides off of a central ring, zipping the sides together along the outside edge, and adding picot embellishments:

RING ROUNDS 1 AND 2: Use 5' (152.5 cm) of thread to string {1C and 1A} sixteen times, leaving a 6" (15 cm) tail. Tie a square knot with the tail and working threads to form a circle. Exit the first C strung (**fig. 4, purple**).

RING ROUND 3: String 1B, skip 1A previously strung, and pass through the next C; repeat to add a total of 16B (**fig. 4, green**). *Note:* Unless otherwise noted, step up for this and each subsequent round by passing through the first bead added in the current round.

RING ROUND 4: Work 1C in each stitch to add a total of 16C (**fig. 4, blue**).

RING ROUND 5: Work 2A in each stitch to add a total of 32A (**fig. 4, red**). Don't step up; exit 1C of Round 4.

RING ROUND 6: Working off of beads in Round 4, work 1C in each stitch to add a total of 16C (**fig. 5, green**). *Note:* Make sure the A of Round 5 remain on the outside of the beadwork when adding the beads of this round.

RING ROUNDS 7 AND 8: Work 1C in each stitch to add a total of 16C in each of 2 rounds (**fig. 5, round 7 in blue; round 8 in red**). *Note:* Work with slightly tighter thread tension in Ring Rounds 6 and 7 so the beadwork cups. Weave through beads to exit 1C of Ring Round 2 (**fig. 5, red**).

RING ROUNDS 9–13: Working the first round off of Ring Round 2, repeat Rounds 3–7. The sides will curl up toward each other.

ZIPPING: Fold the sides up toward each other so that Ring Round 8 meets Ring Round 13 and zip the edges together (**fig. 6, blue**). Repeat the thread path to reinforce. Exit 1C of Ring Round 8.

PICOTS: String 3B and pass through the next C of Round 8 to form a picot (**fig. 6, red**); repeat around the outside edge of the ring to add a picot between each C and a total of 48B. Secure the threads and trim. Set aside.

3 Toggle. Use ladder and tubular herringbone stitches to form the toggle bar:

ROUND 1: Use 6' (183 cm) of thread to ladder-stitch a strip 1A high and 6B long, leaving a 2' (61 cm) tail. Ladder-stitch the first and last beads together to form a ring.

ROUNDS 2–13: Work 3 tubular herringbone stitches with 2B in each stitch to add a total of 6B in each of 12 rounds. *Note:* Step up for each subsequent round by passing through the first bead added in the current round. Join the beads of the last round using a ladder-stitch thread path.

ROUND 14: Work tubular herringbone stitch with 1B in each stitch to add a total of 3B (**fig. 7, green**).

ROUND 15: String 1B and pass through the next B of Round 14; repeat twice. Repeat the thread path to reinforce and exit 1B of Round 14 (**fig. 7, purple**).

FRINGE: String 1C and 1B; pass back through the C to form a fringe and pass through the next B of Round 14 (**fig. 7, red**). Repeat the thread path to reinforce, centering the fringe at the end of the toggle bar. Exit the other end of the toggle bar, from 1 bead of Round 1.

CORE: Use memory wire cutters to cut the paper clips into three ¾" (2 cm) pieces. Tightly tape them together and insert them into the open end of the toggle bar.

ROUNDS 16–17 AND FRINGE: Repeat Rounds 14 and 15 and fringe to complete the other end of the toggle bar. Secure the thread and trim.

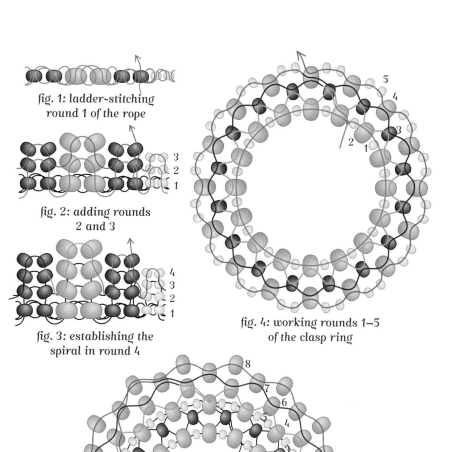

fig. 1: ladder-stitching round 1 of the rope

fig. 2: adding rounds 2 and 3

fig. 3: establishing the spiral in round 4

fig. 4: working rounds 1–5 of the clasp ring

fig. 5: adding rounds 6–8 and weaving through beads to exit round 2

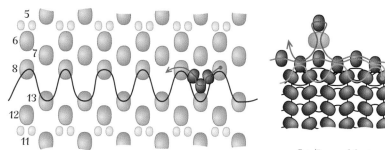

fig. 6: zipping round 13 to round 8 and adding the first picot

fig. 7: working rounds 14 and 15 and adding a fringe at one end of the toggle bar

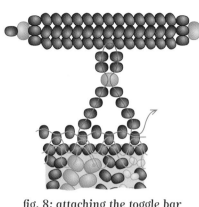

fig. 8: attaching the toggle bar

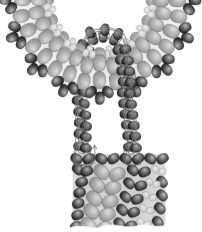

fig. 9: square-stitching a loop that joins the rope and clasp ring

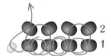

fig. 10: forming rows 1 and 2 of a slider

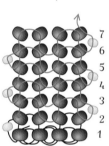

fig. 11: adding rows 3–7

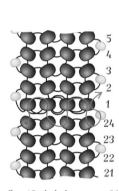

fig. 12: joining row 24 and row 1 to form a ring

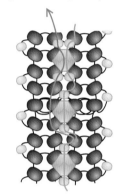

fig. 13: embellishing a slider

5 Clasp ring attachment.

Use square stitch to connect the clasp ring to the starting end of the rope:

Start 2' (61 cm) of new thread that exits from Round 1 of the rope.

END ROUND: Work 1 round of tubular herringbone stitch with 2B in each stitch. Exit from the first 2B added.

LOOP: Square-stitch a strip 2B across and 24 rows long. Pass the strip through the toggle ring and fold the strip so the final beads meet the 2B on the opposite side of the loop start. Making sure the strip isn't twisted, square-stitch the beads together to form a ring **(fig. 9)**. Secure the thread and trim. Set aside.

TIPS

- Because of the dimension the spiral adds to the rope, you'll need to make the rope about 1½" (3.8 cm) longer than you'd usually use for a flat section of beads. Try the rope on as you stitch, remembering that the final rounds and clasp will add 1¾" (4.4 cm).

- In Round 4 of the rope, you'll begin working the step-ups that cause the rope to spiral, but you'll need to bead several rounds before the spiral becomes apparent.

- When working the spiral, the columns will begin to lean to the right. Encourage this movement and tighten each stitch by pulling the thread up to the right.

4 Toggle attachment.

Connect the toggle bar to the end of the rope:

END ROUND 1: Start 2' (61 cm) of new thread that exits from the final round of the rope. Work tubular herringbone stitch with 2B in each stitch to add a total of 8B **(fig. 8, orange)**. *Note:* Unless otherwise noted, step up for this and each subsequent round by passing through the first bead added in the current round.

END ROUND 2: Work tubular herringbone stitch with 1B in each stitch to add a total of 4B **(fig. 8, green)**.

END ROUND 3: String 1B and pass through the next B of End Round 2; repeat three times to add a total of 4B. Don't step up; exit 1B of End Round 2 **(fig. 8, purple)**.

ATTACHMENT: String 4B, 1C, and 2B; pass through 1B at the center of the toggle bar. String 2B; pass back through the last C strung, string 4B, and pass through the B of End Round 2 opposite the one last exited **(fig. 8, red)**. Weave through beads to repeat the thread path twice to reinforce. Secure the thread and trim.

6 Sliders. Use flat herringbone stitch to form the base of the ring-shaped slider, then embellish it with crystals:

ROW 1: Use 3' (91.5 cm) of thread to ladder-stitch a strip 1B high and 4B long. Orient the strip so you're exiting the right end of the beadwork, up through the last bead added (**fig. 10, purple**).

ROW 2: String 2B; pass down through the next B of Row 1 and up through the next B. String 2B; pass down through the next B of Row 1. To work a decorative turnaround, string 1A and pass back through the last B added (**fig. 10, red**).

ROWS 3–24: Repeat Row 2 twenty-two times, continuing to add 1A at each turnaround (**fig. 11, red; Rows 1–7 shown**).

JOIN: Making sure the strip isn't twisted, fold the ends together and stitch Row 24 to Row 1 using a herringbone thread path. Add 1A when turning around at the end of the row as before (**fig. 12**). Weave through beads to reinforce the join.

EMBELLISHMENT ROUND 1: Weave through beads to exit 1 bead in from the edge. String 1A, 1D, and 1A, then skip over 2B in the current column and pass through the next B; repeat seven times along the outside of the ring to add a total of 8D and 16A (**fig. 13, green**).

EMBELLISHMENT ROUND 2: Weave through beads to exit 1B over and 3B up, next to the first A of the next crystal embellishment (**fig. 13, purple**). *String 1A, pass through the nearest D, string 1A, and pass through the nearest B of the current column (**fig. 13, red**). Repeat from * seven times. Secure the thread and trim.
Repeat this entire step three times for a total of 4 sliders. Use the bracelet's toggle bar to string the sliders.

TIPS

- When working the ring sliders, count out 24B before you begin. When beading, take the first bead of each row from that pile—this way when you run out of beads, you know the ring is complete.

- If desired, skip the step-up at the end of Round 4 (and each of the following rounds) to continue in a *down 2, up 1* pattern. The tube will continue to spiral nicely without the step-up.

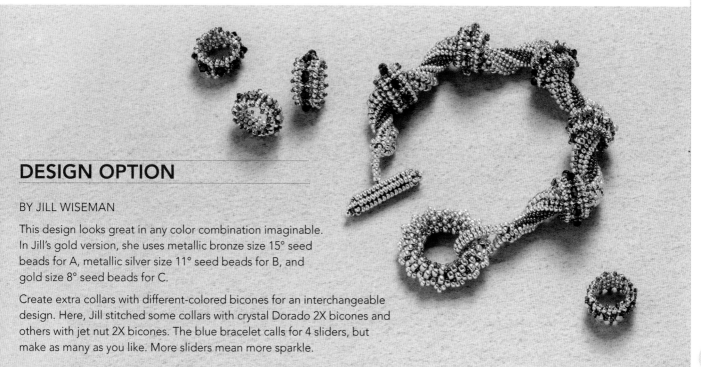

DESIGN OPTION

BY JILL WISEMAN

This design looks great in any color combination imaginable. In Jill's gold version, she uses metallic bronze size 15° seed beads for A, metallic silver size 11° seed beads for B, and gold size 8° seed beads for C.

Create extra collars with different-colored bicones for an interchangeable design. Here, Jill stitched some collars with crystal Dorado 2X bicones and others with jet nut 2X bicones. The blue bracelet calls for 4 sliders, but make as many as you like. More sliders mean more sparkle.

Switch up your step-ups to set your herringbone into a spin. Use accent beads and, if you wish, small sections of peyote stitch to add color and texture as you work the length of this wrapped design. ● by Jean Power

twisty-turny

TECHNIQUES
Ladder stitch

Spiral tubular herringbone stitch

Circular peyote stitch (optional)

Square stitch

MATERIALS
26 g matte gray size 11° seed beads (A)

10 g total accent beads in assorted finishes, sizes, and colors, including 4mm crystal bicones; size 11°, 10°, 8°, 6°, and 3° seed beads; and cylinder beads in dark blue, light blue, turquoise, teal, red, pink, orange, copper, and lime green (B)

Gray size D nylon beading thread

TOOLS
Scissors

Size 12 beading needles

Pliers

FINISHED SIZE
38" (96.5 cm)

fig. 1: ladder-stitching round 1

fig. 2: forming round 2 [flat side view shown for clarity]

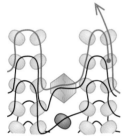

fig. 3: establishing the spiral and adding an accent bead in round 3

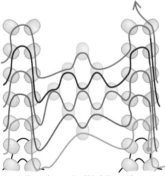

fig. 4: accommodating large accent beads

fig. 5: embellishing the necklace with peyote

fig. 6: stitching the final round of the rope

1 Rope start. Work spiral tubular herringbone stitch with between-column accents to form the necklace:

ROUND 1: Use 6' (183 cm) of thread to ladder-stitch a strip 1A high and 4A long, leaving a 2' (61 cm) tail (**fig. 1, blue**). Ladder-stitch the first and last beads together to form a ring (**fig. 1, red**).

ROUND 2: String 2A, then pass down through the next A of Round 1 and up through the following A of Round 1; repeat. Step up for the next round by passing through the first bead added in the current round (**fig. 2; this and the following figures are shown as flat side views for clarity**).

ROUND 3: String 2A; pass down through the next A of the previous round. String 1B; pass up through the following 2A (A beads of the 2 previous rounds) (**fig. 3, blue**). String 2A; pass down through the next A of the previous round and up through the nearest 3A (A beads of the 2 previous rounds and the first A added in the current round) (**fig. 3, red**). *Note:* The *down 1, up 2* pattern establishes the spiral; think *down 1, up 3* for the second stitch due to the step-up. Notice accent beads are added between the 2 columns only on one side.

2 Rope body, large accents. Repeat Round 3 for the desired length, using the following method when incorporating large accent beads:

In the round that follows a round where you added a large accent bead (crystals and size 8° seed beads and larger), pass through the B of the previous round instead of adding

another B. To do so, string 2A; pass down through the next A of the previous round. Pass through the B added in the previous round and up through the following 2A (A beads of the 2 previous rounds). String 2A; pass down through the next A in the previous round and up through the following 3A (A beads of the 2 previous rounds and the first A added in the current round) (**fig. 4**).

3 Rope body, peyote accents. Repeat Round 3 for the desired length, using the following method when incorporating small diamond-shaped sections of peyote stitch as desired:

PEYOTE ROUND 1: Repeat Round 3, using 1 size 11° seed bead for B (**fig. 5, pink**). *Note:* Use size 11's for B in each of the following rounds, using the same color as the B just placed, if desired.

PEYOTE ROUND 2: String 2A; pass down through the next A of the previous round. String 1B; pass through the B of the previous round. String 1B; pass up through the following 2A (A beads of the 2 previous rounds). String 2A; pass down through the next A of the previous round and up through 3A (A beads of the 2 previous rounds and the first A added in the current round) (**fig. 5, purple**).

PEYOTE ROUND 3: Repeat Peyote Round 2, peyote-stitching 1B before, in between, and after the 2B added in the previous round to add a total of 4A and 3B (**fig. 5, green**).

PEYOTE ROUND 4: Repeat Peyote Round 2, peyote-stitching 1B between each B added in the previous round to add a total of 4A and 2B (**fig. 5, blue**).

PEYOTE ROUND 5: Repeat Peyote Round 2, peyote-stitching 1B between the 2B added in the previous round **(fig. 5, red)**.

4. Toggle. Split the rope and work square stitches off the ends to form the toggle bar:

FINAL ROUND: String 2A; pass down through the next A of the previous round. String 1B; pass up through the following A of the previous round **(fig. 6, blue)**. String 2A; pass down through the next A of the previous round. String 1A; pass up through the following 2A (A of the previous round and the first A added in the current round) **(fig. 6, red)**.

BASE ROWS: String 2A; pass down through the next A of the previous round, then up through the first A of the previous round and the first A just added to form a square stitch. Work

8 more square stitches with 2A in each stitch to add a total of 18A. Work 1 square stitch with 1A, 1B (a size 11° works best here), and 1A for an embellished end **(fig. 7, green)**. Weave through beads to exit 1A in the final round of the rope, opposite the base row just worked **(fig. 7, blue)**. Repeat this entire section to add 9 square stitches with 2A in each stitch and 1 square stitch with 1A, 1B, and 1A as before, exiting an end A **(fig. 7, red)**.

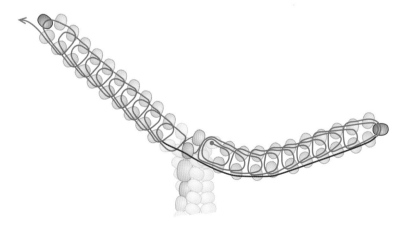

fig. 7: forming the toggle base

TOP, ROW 1: String 1A; pass through the last A exited on the base and the A just added to form a square stitch. Continue square-stitching with 1A in each stitch across the same column of the second half of the base (**fig. 8, green**). Work square stitches into the nearest beads of the final round at the center (**fig. 8, blue**) and continue across the first half of the base row (**fig. 8, red**).

TOP, ROW 2: Repeat Top, Row 1 down the other column on the top of the base.

JOIN: Work back down along Top, Row 2, square-stitching each bead to the nearest bead of Top, Row 1 to close the top of the toggle. Secure the thread and trim.

5 Clasp loop. Add a needle to the tail thread and square-stitch 2A to 2 of the ladder-stitched A of Round 1. Continue square-stitching with 2A in each stitch to form a strip 40 rows long (**fig. 9, blue**). Use a square-stitch thread path to connect the final row of the strip to the 2 remaining ladder-stitched A of Round 1 (**fig. 9, red**). Repeat the thread path of the connection to reinforce. Secure the thread and trim.

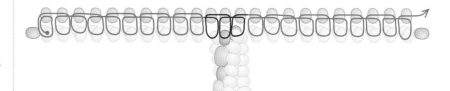

fig. 8: adding top, row 1 to the toggle

fig. 9: creating the clasp loop

TIPS

- Make the rope twist to the right instead of the left by using a *down 2, up 1* pattern.

- Because the piece is long enough to slip over your head, consider going without a clasp and close the ends to form one continuous loop. However, if you plan to wrap the piece around your neck twice, the toggle clasp is a must.

- Wear the beaded rope as a bracelet by wrapping it around your wrist four or five times.

- Size 10° seed beads can be used in place of the size 11°s.

- Anything goes when selecting accent beads. Also try incorporating 2mm and 3mm crystal bicones and rounds. Accent beads smaller than 4mm work best when using size 11° or 10° beads for the rope. For larger accent beads, experiment with making the rope with larger seed beads to maintain proportion.

- This project is a great way to use up leftover beads from other projects. Any color combination looks great for the accent beads when offset with the matte gray herringbone-stitched beads. Since you're not committing to a huge amount of new accent beads, this project presents a great opportunity for exploring new color combinations.

DESIGN OPTION

BY MELINDA BARTA

After falling in love with the way Jean uses just one column of accent beads in her Twisty-Turny necklace (page 114), I had to try a variation of my own. This bangle gets its shape and structure from memory wire and rounds of circular peyote surrounding the end accent beads.

Instead of working Round 1 with ladder stitch, I used a stacked start (see page 80), which incorporated 1 accent bead. The rope was beaded with a *down 2, up 1* pattern (Jean used a *down 1, up 2*), but because I beaded it counterclockwise (looking down from the top of the rope), the rope still twists to the left. Although I am right-handed, sometimes it just feels more natural to stitch counterclockwise than clockwise.

Because all of the between-column accent beads were quite large—size 6° and 8° seed beads, 1.8mm cubes, 3.4mm drops, and a few peanut beads—I followed Jean's technique for incorporating large accent beads (see Step 2 of her Twisty-Turny necklace) every other round. My accent seed beads were actually purchased as a mix, which saved me from needing to make my own "bead soup."

Once the rope reached my desired length, I finished the ends with several rounds of tubular peyote stitch. While stringing the rope onto oval memory wire, I bent the memory wire out of shape. However, once the rope was on the coil of memory wire, I was able to slide it down to an undamaged section of wire. After trimming the memory wire about ¼" (6 mm) from the ends of the rope, I used round-nose pliers to roll each end of the wire down inside the peyote ends. *Note:* Be sure to use memory wire cutters; this wire will damage standard wire cutters. To finish the bracelet and cover the wire ends, I stitched a short fringe of accent beads on each end.

This design features a flat herringbone base joined in the center by five twisted strands that drape beautifully. Multiple flowers in different sizes, accented with curly twisted tendrils, bloom asymmetrically above the strands while a final flower clasp secures the necklace at the back. ● *by Leslie Frazier*

buena vista

TECHNIQUES

Quick-start ladder stitch variation

Circular and flat herringbone stitch

Square stitch

Circular peyote stitch

Tubular right-angle weave

MATERIALS

10 g gold-lined pale gray luster size 11° Japanese seed beads (A)

10 g light raspberry luster size 11° Japanese seed beads (B)

10 g metallic plum iris size 11° Japanese seed beads (C)

15 g satin-finish variegated taupe/silk size 11° cylinder beads (D)

20 g metallic plum iris size 11° Japanese sharp triangles (E)

11 crystal AB 2mm crystal rounds (F)

30 crystal AB 2.5mm crystal bicones (G)

1 crystal AB 3mm crystal round (H)

1 platinum 8mm crystal pearl

Smoke 6 lb braided beading thread

Microcrystalline beading wax

TOOLS

Scissors

Size 11 or 12 beading needles

FINISHED SIZE

31¾" (80.5 cm) (longest strand)

fig. 1: forming the first stitch in row 1 of the short strap

fig. 2: making the second stitch in row 1 of the short strap

fig. 3: adding the first stitch in row 2 of the short strap

fig. 4: stepping up at the end of row 2 of the short strap

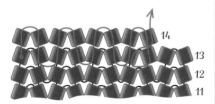

fig. 5: working the decrease in row 14 of the short strap

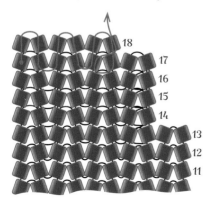

fig. 6: decreasing in row 18 of the short strap

1 Short strap. Use the quick-start ladder stitch variation (page 22) and decreasing flat herringbone stitch to create the short strap for the right side of the necklace, working from the bottom end of the strap toward the end that will feature the clasp flower:

Note: You'll be forming the strap with the back faceup; it will later be flipped so the staggered edge of decreases is on the inside of the necklace.

ROW 1 (QUICK-START LADDER STITCH VARIATION): Add a needle to the center of 8' (244 cm) of thread to double it. Add a stop bead, leaving a 6" (15 cm) tail. String 20E; pass through the seventeenth and eighteenth E just added (**fig. 1**). Pull both the tail and working threads so the last 4E form stacks that are 2 beads high. Pass through the next 2E and pull tight (**fig. 2**); repeat until all of the E sit side by side in 2-bead columns. Remove the stop bead.

ROW 2 (HERRINGBONE STITCH): String 2E, then pass down through the next column of 2E in Row 1 and up through the following 2E (**fig. 3**); repeat three times. For the final stitch of the row, string 2E and pass down through the next column of 2E in Row 1 to add a total of 10E. To step up for the next row, pass up through the 2E closest to the 2E last exited and the last E added (**fig. 4**).

ROWS 3–13: Repeat Row 2 eleven times. *Note:* Unless otherwise noted, use the step-up method shown in **fig. 5** at the end of these and each of the following rows.

ROW 14 (DECREASE): Repeat Row 2, but work only 4 stitches with 2E in each stitch for a total of 8E (**fig. 5**).

ROWS 15–17: Repeat Row 14 three times.

ROW 18 (DECREASE): Repeat Row 2, but work only 3 stitches with 2E in each stitch for a total of 6E (**fig. 6**).

ROWS 19–80: Repeat Row 18 sixty-two times. Secure the threads and trim. Set aside.

2 Long strap and clasp loop. Use a variation of square stitch and decreasing flat herringbone stitch to create the long strap for the left side of the necklace, working from the center of the strap toward the bottom of the strap and then using the tail thread to work out from the center and add the clasp loop:

Note: You'll be forming the strap with the back side faceup; it will later be flipped so the staggered edge of decreases is on the inside of the necklace.

ROW 1: Using 12' (366 cm) of thread and leaving a 2' (61 cm) tail, repeat Step 1, Row 1. *Note:* This row will later be removed; don't tie any knots or split threads.

ROWS 2–24 (HERRINGBONE STITCH): Repeat Step 1, Row 2 twenty-three times.

ROW 25 (DECREASE): Repeat Step 1, Row 2, but work only 4 stitches with 2E in each stitch for a total of 8E.

ROWS 26–34: Repeat Row 25 nine times.

ROW 35 (DECREASE): Repeat Step 1, Row 2, but work only 3 stitches with 2E in each stitch for a total of 6E.

ROWS 36–50: Repeat Row 35 fifteen times.

ROW 51 (DECREASE): Repeat Step 1, Row 2, but work only 2 stitches with 2E in each stitch for a total of 4E.

ROWS 52 AND 53: Repeat Row 51 twice.

ROW 54: Work 1 stitch with 2E. Secure and trim the working thread.

ROW 55: Loosen the tail thread and pull out the beads of Rows 1 and 2. *Note:* The tail thread should exit the bottom-right bead of the work. Rotate the work 180°; the thread will now exit the top left bead of Row 3. Working off of the beads of Rows 3 and 4, string 2E, then pass down through 2E in the next column. Pass up through the nearest E of the first column, then up through 1E of the second column and the second E just added **(fig. 7, green)**. String 1E, then pass down through 2E in the next column and up through the following 2E **(fig. 7, blue)**. Work 3 herringbone stitches with 2E in each stitch, passing down through Rows 3 and 4 in each stitch. To step up for the next row, pass up through the outside E of Row 4, the second E in of Row 3, and the last E just added **(fig. 7, red)**. *Note:* The last bead added in this row should vertically align with the beads added in Row 54 at the bottom end of the strap.

ROW 56 (DECREASE): Repeat Step 1, Row 2, but work only 4 stitches with 2E in each stitch for a total of 8E.

ROW 57: Repeat Row 56.

ROW 58 (DECREASE): Repeat Step 1, Row 2, but work only 3 stitches with 2E in each stitch for a total of 6E.

ROWS 59–116: Repeat Row 58 fifty-eight times.

CLASP LOOP: Exiting the final E of Row 116, string 2B; pass down through the second-to-last E of Row 116, then pass up through the final E of Row 116 and the first B just added **(fig. 8, green)**. *String 2B; pass down through the 2 nearest right-edge beads and up through the 2 adjacent left-edge beads and the first B just added **(fig. 8, blue)**. Repeat from * seventeen times to continue in the *down 2, up 3* pattern until the strip is 19B long. Square-stitch the end of the strip to the first 2E of Row 116 **(fig. 8, red)**. Secure and trim the tail thread. Set aside.

3 **Center strands.** Use a variation of square stitch to form the spiraling strands that join the bottom edges of the straps and form the center of the necklace:

STRAND 1 (INSIDE): Orient the short strap faceup, bottom up, and with the staggered edge of decreases to the right. *Note:* It is easier to work each strand from the bottom up; you'll later rotate the work to match the orientation of **fig. 10** when connecting to the long strap. Start 8' (244 m) of thread that exits from the top right E of Row 1. String 2D and 1A; pass down through the 2E of the next column in Row 1, then up through the nearest outside 2E of Row 1 and first 2D added **(fig. 9, blue)**. *String 1D and 1A; pass down through the previous A in Row 2 and up through the previous 2D and

fig. 7: working row 55 off of row 3 of the long strap

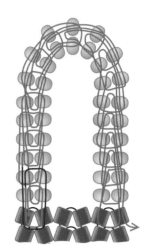

fig. 8: square-stitching the clasp loop

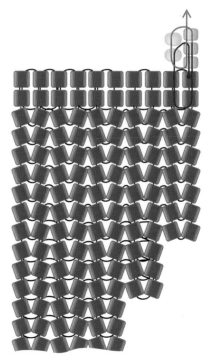

fig. 9: starting strand 1 of the center strands

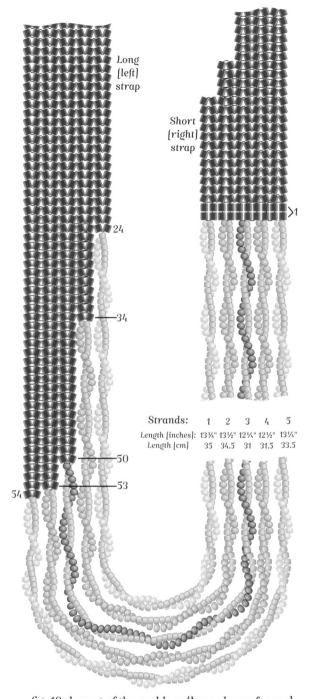

Long
[left]
strap

Short
[right]
strap

24

34

>1

50

53

54

Strands:	1	2	3	4	5
Length [inches]:	13¾"	13½"	12¼"	12½"	13¼"
Length [cm]	35	34.5	31	31.5	33.5

fig. 10: layout of the necklace [base shown faceup]

the D just added (**fig. 9, red**). Repeat from * until the strand measures 13¾" (35 cm). Use tight tension to encourage the strand to twist. Don't trim the thread.

ORIENTATION: Lay both straps on the work surface with the long strap on the left, the short strap on the right, and the ends pointing up; if needed, flip the straps so the staggered decrease edges face each other (these edges will be along the inside of the necklace when worn). Refer to **fig. 10** for strap orientation and the following strand connections.

STRAND 1 CONNECTION: Square-stitch the end of Strand 1 to the beads at the end of the long strap's Row 24. Secure the thread in the strap and trim. *Note:* Make sure the ends aren't twisted here and in the following connections.

STRAND 2: Repeat Strand 1, using B in place of A and starting this strand in the next 2 beads at the end of the short strap. Make this strand 13¼" (33.5 cm) long.

STRAND 2 CONNECTION: Square-stitch the end of Strand 2 to the beads at the end of the long strap's Row 34. Secure the thread and trim.

STRAND 3 (MIDDLE): Repeat Strand 1, using C in place of A and starting this strand in the next 2 beads at the end of the short strap. Make this strand 12¼" (31 cm) long.

STRAND 3 CONNECTION: Square-stitch the end of Strand 3 to the beads at the end of the long strap's Row 50. Secure the thread and trim.

fig. 11: forming the first
3 stitches of the first tendril

fig. 12: cinching the tendril

STRAND 4: Repeat Strand 1, using B in place of A and starting this strand in the next 2 beads at the end of the short strap. Make this strand 12½" (31.5 cm) long.

STRAND 4 CONNECTION: Square-stitch the end of Strand 4 to the beads at the end of the long strap's Row 53. Secure the thread and trim.

STRAND 5 (OUTSIDE): Repeat Strand 1, starting this strand in the final 2 beads at the end of the short strap. Make this strand 13¼" (33.5 cm) long.

STRAND 5 CONNECTION: Square-stitch the end of Strand 5 to the beads at the end of the long strap's Row 54. Secure the thread and trim. Set the necklace base aside.

4 Tendril clusters. Use a variation of square stitch to form a cluster of short twisted strands that will later attach to the straps below the flowers:

BASE: Add a stop bead to the end of 6' (183 cm) of new thread, leaving a 6" (15 cm) tail. Repeat Step 1, Row 1 using D (no need to double the thread as before). Square-stitch the first and last stacks together to form a ring.

TENDRIL: String 2D and 1A; pass down into the next 2D of the base, then up through the 2D just exited and the 2D just added **(fig. 11, blue)**. *String 2D and 1A; pass down through the previous A, then up through the previous D and the 2D just added **(fig. 11, red)**. Repeat from * nineteen times.

CINCHING THE TENDRIL: String 3A; pass back through the second A just strung **(fig. 12, blue)**. String 1A; pass through all the previously added A **(fig. 12, red)**. Pass down

through the column of D in the base next to the starting point and up through the following column. Pull the thread to cause the tendril to curl. Repeat this entire section four times for a total of five tendrils around the base. Secure the threads and trim the tail thread; don't trim the working thread.

Repeat this entire step twice for a total of three tendril clusters. Set aside.

5 Large silver-and-raspberry flower. Use ladder, square, circular herringbone, and circular peyote stitches to form the first large flower:

ROUND 1: Add a stop bead to the end of 6' (183 cm) of new thread, leaving a 6" (15 cm) tail. Repeat Step 1, Row 1 using D (no need to double the thread as before). Square-stitch the first and last stacks together to form a ring.

ROUND 2: String 3D and 1A, then pass down through the next column of 2D in Round 1 to the left and up through the following 2D **(fig. 13)**; repeat four times to add a total of 15D and 5A, forming the base for five petals. Pass up through the first 3D added in this round.

ROUND 3: String 1D and 1A, then pass through the next A of the previous round and up through the top 3D of the next column; repeat four times to add a total of 5D and 5A **(fig. 14, blue)**. *Note:* Always pass up through the top 3D of the next column, even in the last stitch of the round because no step-up is needed at the end of this or the following rounds.

ROUND 4: String 1D and 1A; pass down through the next A of the previous round. String 1A; pass

up through the top 3D of the next column. Repeat from the beginning of this round four times to add a total of 5D and 10A **(fig. 14, red)**.

Note: The work will now begin to spiral. The A between the herringbone columns just added is an increase bead; you'll begin working the sections of peyote off of these beads. As you work, you'll be looking at the back of the flower. The petals will curve out to the left in the first few rounds. Use tight tension throughout to avoid exposed thread and to encourage the petals to curve. Round 1 is the base at the back of the flower; allow the petals to fall away from this base as the beadwork cups.

fig. 13: forming rounds 1 and 2 of the large silver-and-raspberry flower

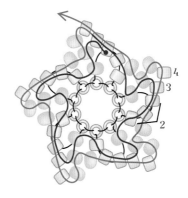

fig. 14: working rounds 3 and 4 of the large silver-and-raspberry flower

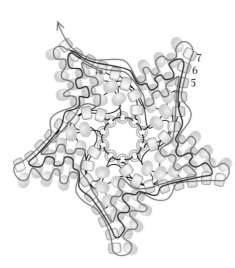

fig. 15: stitching rounds 5–7 of the
large silver-and-raspberry flower

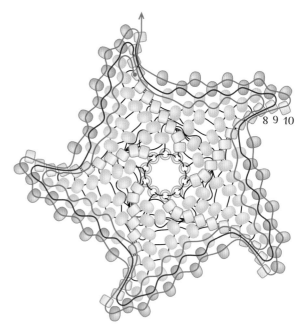

fig. 16: working rounds 8–10 of the large
silver-and-raspberry flower

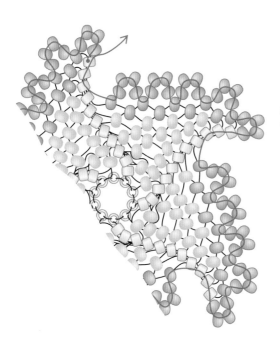

fig. 17: adding the ruffled edge to the large silver-
and-raspberry flower

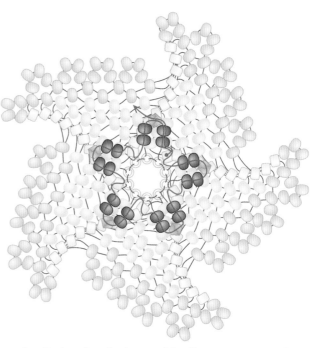

fig. 18: forming the loops of the flower center on the
large silver-and-raspberry flower

ROUND 5: String 1D and 1A; pass down through the next A of the previous round. String 1A; pass through the next A of the previous round (this forms the first circular peyote stitch), then pass up through the top 3D of the next column. Repeat from the beginning of this round four times to add a total of 5D and 10A (**fig. 15, green**).

ROUND 6: String 1D and 1A; pass down through the next A of the previous round. String 1A; pass through the next A of the previous round. String 1A; pass up through the top 3D of the next column. Repeat from the beginning of this round four times to add a total of 5D and 15A (**fig. 15, blue**). *Note:* The petals now begin to curve out to the right.

ROUND 7: String 1D and 1A; pass down through the next A of the previous round. String 1A and pass through the next A of the previous round; repeat. Step up through the top 3D of the next column. Repeat from the beginning of this round four times to add a total of 5D and 15A (**fig. 15, red**).

ROUND 8: String 1D and 1A; pass down through the next A of the previous round. String 1A and pass through the next A of the previous round; repeat. String 1A; pass through the top 3D of the next column. Repeat from the beginning of this round four times to add a total of 5D and 20A (**fig. 16, green**).

ROUND 9: String 1D and 1B; pass down through the next A of the previous round. String 1B and pass through the next A of the previous round; repeat twice. Pass up through the top 3D of the next column. Repeat from the beginning of this round four times to add a total of 5D and 20B (**fig. 16, blue**).

ROUND 10: String 1D and 1B; pass down through the next B of the previous round. String 1B and pass through the next B of the previous round; repeat twice. String 1B; pass up through the top 3D of the next column. Repeat from the beginning of this round four times to add a total of 5D and 25B (**fig. 16, red**).

RUFFLED EDGE: String 4B and pass through the next B of the previous round to form a loop; repeat four times. Pass up through the top 3D of next column. Repeat from the beginning of this round four times to add a total of 20 loops (100B) (**fig. 17**).

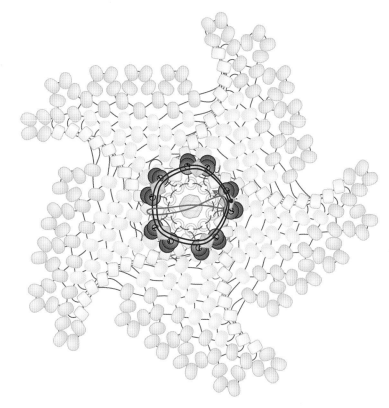

fig. 19: completing the flower center

FLOWER CENTER: Flip the work over. Weave through beads to exit through the flower center from the first D added in Round 2. *Note:* The following beads will be added on the topside of the flower; to double-check the orientation, the petal tips will curve to the left on the topside. *String 2C, 1G, and 2C; pass up through the nearest D (of Round 2, 3, or 4, whichever is easiest to access) in the next column, away from the center of the flower to form a loop. Repeat from * four times to add a total of 20C and 5G. Step up through the first 2C and 1G added in this round (**fig. 18**). Pass through all 5G twice to form a circle and pull the loops toward the center (**fig. 19, blue**). String 1H; skip 2G of the circle and pass the needle under the thread connecting the Gs. Pass back through the H just

added (**fig. 19, red**). Repeat the thread path to reinforce. Secure and trim the tail thread; don't trim the working thread. Set aside.

6 *Extra-large raspberry-and-silver flower.* Use ladder, square, circular herringbone, and circular peyote stitches to form the second large flower:

ROUNDS 1–8: Repeat Step 5, Rounds 1–8, using B in place of A.

ROUNDS 9 AND 10: Repeat Step 5, Rounds 9 and 10.

ROUND 11: String 1D and 1A; pass down through the next B of the previous round. String 1A and pass through the next B of the previous round; repeat three times. Pass up through the top 3D of the next column. Repeat from the beginning of this round four times to add a total of 5D and 25A. Step up through

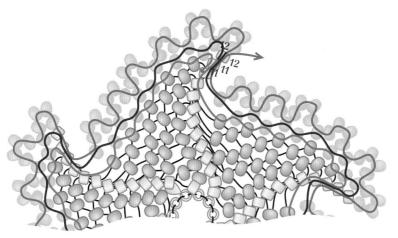

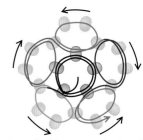

fig. 20: working rounds 11 and 12 and the ruffled edge of the extra-large raspberry-and-silver flower

fig. 21: stitching rounds 1 and 2 of the beaded button

the first bead added in this round (fig. 20, green).

ROUND 12: String 1D and 1A; pass down through the next A of the previous round. String 1A and pass through the next A of the previous round; repeat three times. String 1A; pass up through the top 3D of the next column. Repeat from the beginning of this round four times to add a total of 5D and 30A (fig. 20, blue).

RUFFLED EDGE: String 4A and pass through the next A of the previous round to form a loop; repeat five times. Pass up through the top 3D of the next column. Repeat from the beginning of this round four times to add a total of 30 loops (120A) (fig. 20, red).

FLOWER CENTER: Repeat Step 5, Flower Center, using 1G in place of the centermost H.

7 *Medium silver-and-plum flower.* Repeat Step 5, making changes where indicated: Repeat Rounds 1–8. Repeat Round 9 using C in place of B. Skip Round 10. Repeat Ruffled Edge,

working off of the beads in Round 9, using C in place of B, adding a loop at the tip of each column, and forming 3 loops between each column to add a total of 20 loops (80C). Repeat Flower Center, using 1G in place of the centermost H.

8 *Small plum-and-silver flower.* Repeat Step 5, making changes where indicated: Repeat Round 1. Repeat Round 2 using C in place of A. Skip Round 3. Repeat Rounds 4–6 using C in place of A. Skip Rounds 7–10. Repeat Ruffled Edge, working off of the beads in Round 6, using A in place of B, adding 1 loop at the tip of each column, and forming 2 loops between each column to add a total of 15 loops (60C). Repeat Flower Center using B in place of C and F in place of G, and 1G in place of the centermost H.

9 *Small silver-and-raspberry flower.* Repeat Step 5, making changes where indicated: Repeat Round 1–6. Skip Rounds 7–10. Repeat Ruffled Edge, working off of the beads in Round 6, adding 1 loop at the tip of each column, and forming 2 loops

between each column to add a total of 15 loops (60B). Repeat Flower Center, using 1G in place of the centermost H.

10 *Small raspberry flower.* Repeat Step 5, making changes where indicated: Repeat Round 1. Repeat Rounds 2–6 using B in place of A. Skip Rounds 7–10. Repeat Ruffled Edge, working off of the beads in Round 6, adding 1 loop at the tip of each column, and forming 2 loops between each column to add a total of 15 loops (60B). Repeat Flower Center, using 1G in place of the centermost H.

11 *Small silver-and-raspberry clasp flower.* Use 6' (183 cm) of thread to string 5B, leaving a 6" (15 cm) tail; tie a knot to form a tight circle and exit the first B. Stitch 1D and 1A between each B of the starting ring; step up through the first D added. Repeat Step 5, making changes where indicated: Repeat Rounds 2–6. Repeat Round 7 using B in place of A. Skip Rounds 8–10. Repeat Ruffled Edge, working off of the beads in Round 6, adding 1 loop at the tip of

TIPS

- The beauty of working flat herringbone stitch with triangles is that they naturally "pop" into place. This means you'll begin to see columns where the triangle points align and, in the next column, the flat sides will all point in the same direction.

- Keep the tension even throughout the center strands to avoid interrupting the smooth twists.

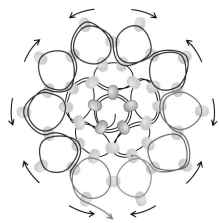

fig. 22: working round 3 of the beaded button

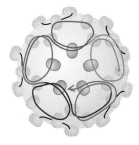

fig. 23: securing the pearl and beading round 5 of the beaded button

each column, and forming 3 loops between each column to add a total of 15 loops (60B). Repeat Flower Center, using 1G in place of the centermost H. Secure and trim the working and tail threads.

12 Beaded button. Use tubular right-angle weave to form the clasp button for the end of the short strap:

ROUND 1: Use 3' (91.5 cm) of thread to string 5B, leaving a 6" (15 cm) tail. Pass through the 5B again to form a tight circle; exit from the first B strung (**fig. 21, black**).

ROUND 2, UNIT 1: String 4A; pass through the B just exited and up through the first A added in this unit (**fig. 21, turquoise**).

ROUND 2, UNIT 2: String 3A; pass back through the next B of Round 1, up through the nearest side A of the previous unit, and through the 3A just added and the next B of Round 1 (**fig. 21, purple**).

ROUND 2, UNIT 3: String 3A; pass down through the nearest side A of the previous unit, through the B of Round 1 just exited, and up through the first A added in this unit (**fig. 21, green**).

ROUND 2, UNIT 4: Repeat Unit 2 (**fig. 21, blue**).

ROUND 2, UNIT 5: Pass up through the nearest side A of Unit 1. String 2A; pass down through the nearest side A of the previous unit and weave through beads to exit the first bead added in this unit (**fig. 21, red**).

ROUND 3, UNIT 1: String 3A; pass through the last A exited and up through the first A just added (**fig. 22, turquoise**).

ROUND 3, UNIT 2: String 2A; pass back through the next A of Round 2, the nearest A in the previous unit, the 2C just added, and the following A of Round 2 (**fig. 22, purple**).

ROUND 3, UNIT 3: String 2A; pass down through the nearest A of the previous unit, the next A of Round 2, and up through the first A just added (**fig. 22, green**).

ROUND 3, UNITS 4–9: Repeat Units 2 and 3 three times (**fig. 22, blue**).

ROUND 3, UNIT 10: String 1A; pass down through the nearest A in Unit 1 of Round 3, through the open A in Round 2, up through the nearest A in Unit 9 of Round 3, and through the A just added (**fig. 22, red**).

ROUND 4: Repeat Round 3, using A to form a 4-bead unit off of the top of each unit in Round 3.

ROUND 5, UNIT 1: Insert the 8mm pearl and hold it against the beadwork as you work the following round. Pass through the next A of Round 4. String 1A, 1B, and 1A; pass through the last 2A exited and up through the first A just added (**fig. 23, turquoise**).

ROUND 5, UNIT 2: String 1B and 1A; pass back through the next 2A of Round 4, up through the nearest A in the previous unit, and through the B/A just added and the following 2A of Round 4 (**fig. 23, purple**).

ROUND 5, UNIT 3: String 1A and 1B; pass down through the nearest A of the previous unit, through the next 2A of Round 4, and up through the first A just added (**fig. 23, green**).

ROUND 5, UNIT 4: Repeat Unit 2 (**fig. 23, blue**).

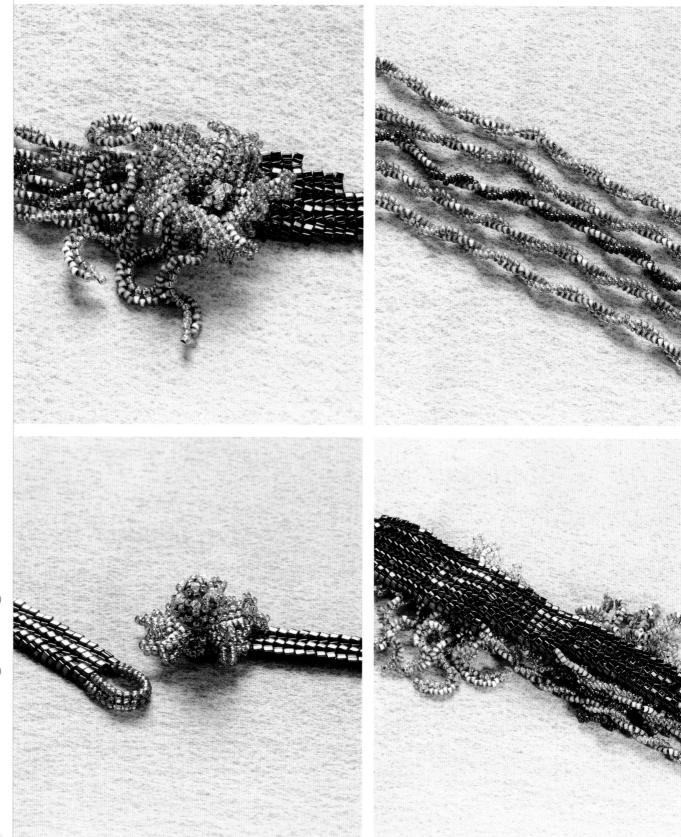

ROUND 5, UNIT 5: Pass up through the nearest side A of Unit 1. String 1B; pass down through the nearest side A of the previous unit and weave through beads to exit 1B **(fig. 23, red)**. Pass up through each B added in this unit twice to enclose the pearl.

EMBELLISHMENT: Weave through beads to exit one side A of Round 5, toward the center ring of B. String 1F and pass through the next side A of Round 5, toward the center; repeat four times to add a total of 5F. Pass through the nearest B of Round 5. String 1F; pass through the opposite B of Round 5, pass back through the F just added, and through the next B of Round 5 **(fig. 24)**. Weave through the embellishment beads again to reinforce the thread path, then weave through beads to exit Round 1.

BUTTON STEM: String 1B; pass through a B in Round 1 of the clasp flower from Step 11. *Note:* Don't flip the clasp flower; the petals should curve to the right. String 1B; pass through the last B exited in the button's Round 1, the first B just added, and the next B in Round 1 of the clasp flower. Continue using tubular right-angle weave and B to join Round 1 of the button to Round 1 of the clasp flower.

CONNECTION: Orient the necklace base faceup, with the short strap on the right, the long strap on the left, and the staggered edge of decreases on the inside edge of the necklace. Sew Round 1 of the clasp flower to the front of the short strap, ½" (1.3 cm) from the end of the short strap.

13 **Assembly:** Orient the necklace base faceup, with the short strap on the right, the long strap on the left, and the staggered edge of decreases on the inside of the necklace. Use the remaining working threads to sew Round 1 of the flowers and tendrils to the front of the necklace base, positioning them as desired or following this placement:

LARGE SILVER-AND-RASPBERRY FLOWER: Sew this flower ½" (1.3 cm) from the bottom edge of the short (right) strap.

SMALL SILVER-AND-RASPBERRY FLOWER: Sew this flower ½" (1.3 cm) from the bottom edge of the long (left) strap.

MEDIUM SILVER-AND-PLUM FLOWER: Sew this flower 1¼" (3.2 cm) from the bottom edge of the long (left) strap. Allow the petals of this flower to overlap the previous ones.

SMALL RASPBERRY FLOWER: Sew this flower 2" (5 cm) from the bottom edge of the long (left) strap.

EXTRA-LARGE RASPBERRY-AND-SILVER FLOWER: Sew this flower 3" (7.5 cm) from the bottom edge of the long (left) strap.

SMALL PLUM-AND-SILVER FLOWER: Sew this flower 4¼" (11 cm) from the bottom edge of the long (left) strap.

TENDRIL CLUSTERS: Sew one tendril cluster under the large silver-and-raspberry flower's bottom petals, with the tendrils falling down away from the flower and covering the strand connections. *Note:* Tuck the base of each tendril cluster under a flower petal to conceal the base row. Sew one tendril cluster between the medium silver-and-plum and small raspberry flowers, with the tendrils falling away from the center of the necklace. Sew the remaining tendril cluster under the top petals of the extra-large raspberry-and-silver flower, with the tendrils falling toward the center of the necklace. Secure and trim all remaining threads.

TIPS

- If needed, use chain-nose pliers throughout the project to help maneuver the needle through the beads.

- When sewing the flowers to the strap, hold the flower in place and weave up between triangle beads into the center area of the flower, into a column of cylinder beads. Weave down through adjacent cylinder beads and pass through the necklace strap to the back. Weave through triangle beads to another area behind the same flower and repeat the sewing technique until the flower is secure.

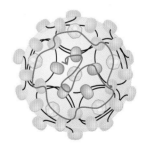

fig. 24: embellishing the beaded button

finishing touches

For many beaders, no project feels complete without an extra layer of decoration. Study the various embellishment techniques in the how-tos and projects that follow and discover how combining herringbone with other stitches opens up a world of design possibilities.

In my **Anything Goes** bracelet, you'll master the art of adding between-column embellishment beads, in-column and between-column fringe, and large mid-rope accent beads. Plus, learn how a bit of basic wireworking finishes the rope ends with a professional and contemporary look.

Clever embellishment loops give the appearance of circular herringbone stitch in Lisa Kan's bold origami-inspired neckpiece, **Girasole**. With the backs beaded from the inside outward and the fronts beaded from the outside inward, Lisa's unique construction technique for the rings is one you must try.

Stitch short sections of curved tubular herringbone rope into playfully arranged components for my **Paisley Paillettes** bracelet. Simple stitch-in-the-ditch embellishments add a finishing touch, as do the faceted rondelles that adorn the center of each paisley and the small fringes at the tips. Also see my variation on the design, **Semiprecious Paisley Necklace**.

TECHNIQUES

fringe

Use this versatile and easy-to-bead technique to add texture to any project.

BASIC FRINGE

To form a fringe, string 1 or more decorative beads and 1 bead for the tip. Skip the bead used for the tip, then pass back through the decorative bead(s) (**fig. 1, blue**). If using crystals for the decorative beads, consider stringing 1 small bead before the crystal (**fig. 1, red**); this will help protect the thread from being accidentally cut by the often-sharp edge of the crystal.

To tighten the fringe, pull up on the bead at the tip to snug the decorative bead down to the beadwork and then pull the thread gently to remove the rest of the slack.

IN-COLUMN FRINGE

Fringe can be added while stitching any row or round. To position a fringe within a column, string the first bead of the herringbone pair, 1 decorative bead, and 1 bead for the tip of the fringe. Skip the tip bead, then pass back through the decorative bead and string the second bead of the herringbone pair (**fig. 2, blue**). To complete the herringbone stitch, pass through the next bead of the previous row/round and up through the following bead of the previous row/round (**fig. 2, red**). When working subsequent rows/rounds, make sure the fringe falls toward the front of the work.

BETWEEN-COLUMN FRINGE

Fringe can also be added between columns while working across any row or round. String the herringbone pair and pass through

the next bead of the previous row/round (**fig. 3, blue**). Before passing up through the following bead of the previous row/round as usual, add the fringe: String 1 decorative bead and 1 bead for the tip of the fringe; skip the tip bead, then pass back through the decorative bead and up through the next bead of the previous row/round to complete the herringbone stitch (**fig. 3, red**). Be sure to position the fringe on the front of the work when working the following rows/rounds.

LOOP FRINGE

Work decorative loops at the end of the final row/round by stringing any number of beads, skipping over as few or as many beads as desired, and passing through the next end bead. Adjust the number of beads in each loop and the number of beads skipped in the final row/round to achieve the desired look (**fig. 4**). Loops can be worked anywhere along the beadwork to add dimension and texture. You may also hear a loop of beads referred to as a net.

stitch-in-the-ditch embellishment

Layers of decoration can be easily added on top of previously stitched rows/rounds of beadwork. Exit 1 bead in the row/round you wish to embellish, string 1 decorative bead, and pass through the next bead in an adjacent row/round. Repeat as desired (**fig. 5**). In herringbone, this often looks best when embellishing with beads that are smaller than those used for the base. When traveling from 1 herringbone bead to the next, follow a previous thread path to avoid exposed threads.

When adding this type of embellishment to the outside

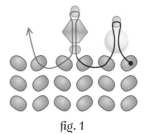

fig. 1

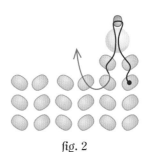

fig. 2

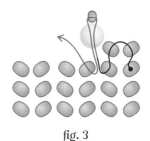

fig. 3

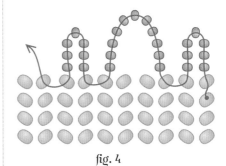

fig. 4

fig. 5

fig. 6

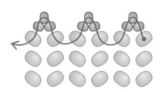

fig. 8

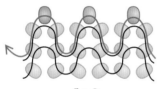

fig. 9

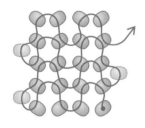

fig. 10

edge of a tubular herringbone rope, follow a zigzag/stairstep pattern (**fig. 6**).

picot embellishment

Picots are most commonly used for decorative edges, but they can be added to any part of a project to give extra texture and a bit of frill.

BASIC PICOT

Work the final row/round of flat, circular, or tubular herringbone stitch with 3 beads in each stitch. Use tight tension so the center bead juts out from the other two. For contrast, use beads for the picots that are smaller than the beads of the base (**fig. 8**).

By retracing the thread path of the final row/round and adding 1 bead between each of the herringbone pairs, you can achieve the look of picots due to the natural angle of herringbone pairs and the protrusion of the top beads of each column (**fig. 9**).

edge embellishment

Revisit the decorative turnarounds in the Flat Herringbone technique section (page 28) to see how beads can be added along the outside edges of the beadwork as you work row by row (**fig. 10**).

peyote combinations

Take your herringbone skills to the next level by learning how to seamlessly transition from this stitch to and from peyote.

HERRINGBONE-TO-PEYOTE TRANSITION

To work peyote stitch off of herringbone stitch, work the final row/round of herringbone with 1 bead in each stitch (**fig. 11, blue**). Then work peyote stitch off of the last row/round of beads, stitching 1 bead between each previous bead (**fig. 11, red**). Alternatively, you could work the final row/round of herringbone with 3 beads in each stitch and pass through only the center bead at the top of each column when adding the first row/round of peyote.

The example shown will cause the beadwork to decrease along the top edge, making it a perfect way to close a herringbone-stitched bezel. If you want the work to remain flat, use larger beads or more beads in each peyote stitch.

PEYOTE-TO-HERRINGBONE TRANSITION

To transition from peyote to herringbone stitch, begin by working a row/round with 2 beads in each stitch (**fig. 12, green**).

To stitch the second row/round, work herringbone stitch with 2 beads in each stitch (**fig. 12, blue**).

If the herringbone section is narrower than the peyote section, you can control the shaping by adding 1 or more beads between each herringbone column (**fig. 12, red**).

square-stitch combination

Square stitch is a great partner to herringbone because of the way it aligns beads side by side, similar to the way herringbone does. It's perfect for making coordinating clasp loops.

See page 159 for how to form a square-stitch strip off of a pair of herringbone beads.

You can also work square stitch off of the side of a herringbone piece (**fig. 13**). This can come in handy when attaching a finding or another piece of beadwork.

brick-stitch combination

See page 57 for how to establish a base of brick stitch around a focal bead. This method perfectly aligns the beads for the herringbone rounds that follow.

If incorporating herringbone stitch into bead embroidery, brick stitch is the ideal choice for the starting row/round. Tie a couple of strong overhand knots at the end of 3' (91.5 cm) of thread and place a needle at the other end. Pass through the bead-embroidery foundation from back to front. String 2 beads and slide them down to the foundation. Pass down through the foundation 2 beads' width away from the starting point. Pass back up through the foundation very close to where the thread is exiting to make a small stitch and then pass back up through the last bead added. Pull the thread snug to position the beads side by side (fig. 14, blue).

*String 1 bead and pass down through the foundation, 1 bead's width away from the previous bead. Pass back up through the foundation very close to where the thread is exiting to make a small stitch, then pass back up through the last bead added. Pull the thread snug to position the new bead next to the previous one (fig. 14, red). Repeat from * to continue the row/round. If working in rounds, join the final bead to the first bead using the same brick-stitch thread path. Make sure the total number of beads in the row/round is an even number. Pass up through one of the brick stitches and begin herringbone stitch.

fig. 11

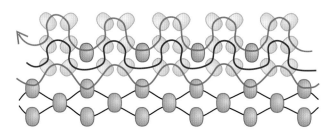

fig. 12

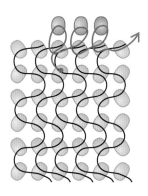

fig. 13

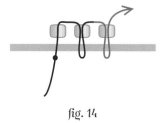

fig. 14

Thread embellishment

Here's a great way to add embellishment beads that I picked up from Maggie Meister. Instead of passing through any of the previously added beads in a project, add embellishments to the thread loops that connect the beads of the herringbone base. In this example, beads are added along the outside edge of a tubular herringbone rope. Exit 1 edge bead, *string 1 embellishment bead, and pass the needle under the next herringbone thread loop to catch the thread. Repeat from * (fig. A).

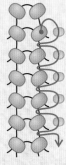

fig. A

135

Use a funky mix of beads to make a tactile bracelet that's as fun to stitch as it is to wear. The instructions take you bead by bead, round by round through Round 35 to teach you various embellishment techniques. From there on out, it's "anything goes"!
● by *Melinda Barta*

anything goes

TECHNIQUES
Ladder stitch

Tubular herringbone stitch

Fringe

Wireworking

MATERIALS
0.5 g matte metallic light yellow/green iris size 15° seed beads (A)

2 g matte metallic cabernet iris size 11° Japanese seed beads (B)

3 g matte metallic olive-gold size 11° Japanese seed beads (C)

1 g citrine-lined emerald size 11° Japanese seed beads (D)

2 g matte silver size 11° Japanese seed beads (E)

2 g matte robin's egg blue 4×2mm peanut beads (F)

3 g matte metallic red copper iris 3.4mm drops (G)

3 g metallic brown iris 3.4mm drops (H)

3 total 12mm raku rounds in purple, brown, and pale mustard yellow (I)

1 blue striped 13×11mm ceramic rondelle

2 antiqued copper 10×11mm end caps

1 bronze 13×21mm clasp hook

8" (20.5 cm) of dark copper 20-gauge craft wire

Smoke 6 lb braided beading thread

TOOLS
Scissors

Size 10 beading needles

Wire cutters

FINISHED SIZE
8⅞" (22.7 cm)

NOTE
The instructions are for the silver, green, and purple colorway. For information on the orange, magenta, and purple colorway, see page 141.

fig. 1: forming round 1

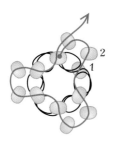

fig. 2: adding round 2

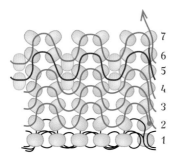

fig. 3: working rounds 3–7

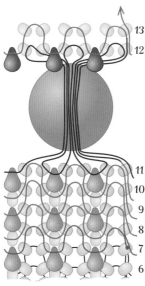

fig. 4: stitching rounds 8–13 and incorporating the first large accent bead

1 Rope start. Use tubular herringbone stitch to form the starting end of the rope:

ROUND 1: Use 6' (183 cm) of thread to ladder-stitch a strip 1E high and 6E long, leaving a 6" (15 cm) tail **(fig. 1, blue)**. Ladder-stitch the first and last beads together to form a ring **(fig. 1, red)**.

ROUND 2: String 2E, then pass down through the next E of Round 1 and up through the following E of Round 1; repeat twice. *Note:* Step up for this and each subsequent round by passing through the first bead added in the current round **(fig. 2)**.

ROUNDS 3–5: Work tubular herringbone stitch with 2E in each stitch to add a total of 6E in each of 3 rounds **(fig. 3, green; this and the following figures are shown as flat side views for clarity)**.

ROUND 6: String 2E; pass down through the next E of the previous round. String 1C; pass up through the following E of the previous round. Repeat from the beginning of this round twice to add a total of 6E and 3C **(fig. 3, blue)**.

ROUND 7: Repeat Round 6 **(fig. 3, red)**.

2 Rope body, first half. Use tubular herringbone stitch to form the rope, incorporating fringe and other embellishments along the way:

ROUND 8: String 2E; pass down through the next E of the previous round. String 1H; pass up through the following E of the previous round. Repeat from the beginning of this round twice to add a total of 6E and 3H **(fig. 4, purple)**.

ROUNDS 9–11: Repeat Round 6, Round 8, and then Round 6 **(fig. 4, green)**. *Note:* When working rounds that follow rounds with drop beads (G and H), make sure the bulbous ends of the drops fall to the outside of the rope.

ROUND 12 (BEGIN FIRST OLIVE SECTION): String 1 brown I and 2C, then pass back through the I and the next E of Round 11. String 1H and pass up through the following E of the previous round. Repeat from the beginning of this round twice, passing through the first I strung instead of stringing another I, to add a total of 1I, 6C, and 3H **(fig. 4, blue)**. *Note:* See the tip on page 139 if the C beads slip down through the I.

ROUND 13: String 2C; pass down through the next C of the previous round. String 1G; pass up through the following C of the previous round. Repeat from the beginning of this round twice to add a total of 6C and 3G **(fig. 4, red)**.

FRINGE: Pass down through the next C of Round 13, the nearest C of Round 12, and the I, then pass up through the nearest E of Round 11 to exit toward the I. *String 1F and 1A, then pass back through the F to form a fringe. Pass through the nearest E/H/E. Repeat from * twice to add a total of 3 fringes **(fig. 5, blue)**. Pass through the I and 1C of Round 12. **String 1F and 1A, then pass back through the F to form a fringe. Pass through the nearest C/G/C. Repeat from ** twice to add a total of 3 fringes. Pass through the nearest C in Round 13 **(fig. 5, red)**.

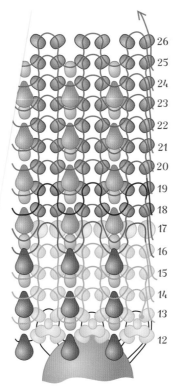

fig. 6: working rounds 14–26

[...] 13. [...] the following [...] eat from the beginning of this round twice to add a total of 6C and 3D **(fig. 6, pink)**.

ROUNDS 15 AND 16: Repeat Rounds 13 and 14 **(fig. 6, orange)**.

ROUND 17 (PEANUT ROUND): String 2F; pass down through the next C of the previous round. String 1G; pass up through the following C of the previous round. Repeat from the beginning of this round twice to add a total of 6F and 3G. Adjust the peanuts so one bulbous half of each bead points to the center of the rope and the other half points out **(fig. 6, purple)**.

ROUND 18 (BEGIN FIRST CABERNET SECTION): String 2B; pass down through the next bead of the previous round.

String 1D; pass up through the following bead of the previous round. Repeat from the beginning of this round twice to add a total of 6B and 3D **(fig. 6, green)**.

ROUND 19: String 2B; pass down through the next B of the previous round. String 1H; pass up through the following B of the previous round. Repeat from the beginning of this round twice to add a total of 6B and 3H **(fig. 6, blue)**.

ROUNDS 20–26: Repeat Rounds 18 and 19 three times. Repeat Round 18 **(fig. 6, red)**.

ROUND 27 (IN-COLUMN FRINGE): String 1B, 1F, and 1A; pass back through the F to form a fringe. String 1B; pass down through the next B of the previous round. String 1H; pass up through the following B of the previous round. Repeat from the beginning of this round

TIPS

- You can work several rounds and later add fringe (as in Step 2, Fringe) or work the fringe right into the stitch, as in Rounds 27 and 29.

- Copper craft wire can be soft, so choose a gauge that's strong enough (at least 20-gauge) to act as the clasp loop.

- If the size 11° seed beads added above the ceramic rounds slip down through the hole, here are three ways you can solve the problem:

  1. Before stringing the beads that will sit above the ceramic round, string enough beads to fill the core of the round. You'll just need to make sure you pass back and forth through all of these core beads as you stitch. Because of the number of passes, you'll need to switch to a thinner needle.

  2. Temporarily string the 6 size 11°s that will sit on top of the ceramic bead on 6" (15 cm) of thread; don't tie a knot. Pass through 2 of the 6 beads at a time in each of the 3 stitches (instead of stringing new ones above the ceramic round), making sure you don't split the temporary thread. Remove the temporary thread once you're ready to start the following round.

  3. This is the method I used for this project: Temporarily hold the beads that will sit above the ceramic round with a second needle. Leave them on the second needle as long as possible, ideally until you're ready to work the following round. This method is much like holding stitches on a needle when knitting.

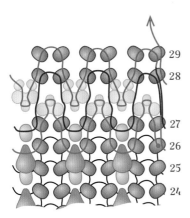

fig. 7: forming rounds 27–29

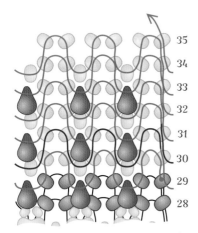

fig. 8: stitching rounds 30–35

fig. 9: finishing an end

twice to add a total of 6B, 3 F/A fringes, and 3H **(fig. 7, green)**.

ROUND 28: Repeat Round 18 **(fig. 7, blue)**.

ROUND 29 (BETWEEN-COLUMN FRINGE): String 2B; pass down through the next B of the previous round. String 1A, 1F, and 1A; pass back through the F to form a fringe, string 1A, and pass up through the following B of the previous round. Repeat from the beginning of this round twice to add a total of 6B, 3 F/A fringes, and 6A that sit under the fringe **(fig. 7, red)**.

ROUND 30 (BEGIN SECOND SILVER SECTION): String 2E; pass down through the next bead of the previous round. String 1G; pass up through the following bead of the previous round. Repeat from the beginning of this round twice to add a total of 6E and 3G. *Note:* Make sure the fringes of Round 29 are on the outside of the rope **(fig. 8, green)**.

ROUND 31: String 2E; pass down through the next E of the previous round. String 1C; pass up through the following E of the previous round. Repeat from the beginning of this round twice to add a total of 6E and 3C **(fig. 8, blue)**.

ROUNDS 32–35: Repeat Rounds 30 and 31 twice **(fig. 8, red)**.

3 Rope, second half. Continue in embellished tubular herringbone stitch:

ROPE: Continue working the length of the rope to the desired length, minus 2" (5 cm) for the closure, in the color combinations of your choice, adding the remaining accent beads (purple and yellow rounds and the striped rondelle) following the technique used in Rounds 10–13. Repeat Round 17 to replace the size 11°s used for the herringbone columns with peanut beads (F) as desired. Add fringe using the technique in Step 2, Fringe, or add fringe in-column as in Round 27 or between-column as in Round 29.

END: To make the second end mirror the first, work 2 rounds with only size 11° accent beads between columns. Work 2 rounds without adding any accent beads between columns. Weave through beads to exit the third-to-last round.

4 Assembly. Use simple wireworking techniques to finish the ends of the rope:

INNER LOOP: Use 4" (10 cm) of wire to form a small wrapped loop, making sure the loop is small enough to fit into the ends of the rope. Slightly flatten the loop into an oval shape, if needed. Stitch the loop in place, securing it by passing back and forth from one side of the rope to the other **(fig. 9, red)**. Secure the thread and trim. (See this technique illustrated on page 83.)

END: Use the wire to string 1 end cap (wide end first) down over the end of the rope. Form a second wrapped loop that connects to the clasp hook **(fig. 9)**.

Repeat this entire step on the other end of the rope, using the tail thread to secure the inner loop and making the end loop large enough (about ¼" [6 mm]) to accommodate the hook clasp.

DESIGN OPTIONS

BY MELINDA BARTA

- For the warmer-colored bracelet on page 136, start with mauve, red, and orange ceramic rounds and pair them with purple, magenta, and orange hues of matte size 11° seed beads. Find coordinating matte and shiny drops and peanut beads for the embellishments and finish the ends with bright copper caps, 20-gauge copper wire, and a copper clasp hook. The single cream-and-red polka-dotted ceramic round adds a bit of whimsy.

- Instead of splitting up sections of the rope with large accent beads that all the columns connect to, add a break in the action with a long, oval-shaped accent bead in each column. The samples below also show what happens when you omit the peanut bead fringes.

The inspiration for this stunning neckpiece comes from Ring of Rings, an origami sculpture of interlocking paper rings by U.S. paper artist Mette Pederson. Be amazed by the construction methods behind Lisa's flowerlike embellishment that led to the project's name, Girasole, Italian for "sunflowers."
● *by Lisa Kan*

girasole

TECHNIQUES
Tubular and twisted tubular herringbone stitch

Tubular peyote stitch

Picot

Zipping

MATERIALS
40 g topaz bronze luster size 15° Japanese seed beads (A)

3 g green iris size 15° Japanese seed beads (B)

3 g blue hematite size 15° Japanese seed beads (C)

3 g purple iris size 15° Japanese seed beads (D)

3 g raspberry bronze iris size 15° Japanese seed beads (E)

3 g blue iris size 15° Japanese seed beads (F)

3 g purple hematite size 15° Japanese seed beads (G)

5 g green iris size 11° Japanese seed beads (H)

5 g blue hematite size 11° Japanese seed beads (I)

5 g purple iris size 11° Japanese seed beads (J)

5 g raspberry bronze iris size 11° Japanese seed beads (K)

5 g blue iris size 11° Japanese seed beads (L)

5 g purple hematite size 11° Japanese seed beads (M)

1 heliotrope 6mm 8-petal crystal marguerite flower

2¼" (5.5 cm) of bronze 18-gauge craft wire

Smoke 6 lb braided beading thread

TOOLS
Scissors

Size 12 beading needles

Wire cutters

FINISHED SIZE
19½" (49.5 cm)

1 **Green ring, back.** Use tubular peyote stitch, picots, and green and bronze beads to form the back of the first ring:

ROUNDS 1 AND 2: Use 7' (213 cm) of thread to string 50H, leaving a 6" (15 cm) tail. Tie a square knot with the tail and working threads to form a circle. Exit the first bead added, making sure the knot doesn't slip inside the bead (**fig. 1, purple**).

ROUND 3: String 1H, skip 1H previously strung, and pass through the next H; repeat twenty-four times to add a total of 25H (**fig. 1, blue**). *Note:* Unless otherwise noted, step up for this and each subsequent round by passing through the first bead added in the current round. To keep the beadwork flexible, use relaxed thread tension.

ROUND 4: Work tubular peyote stitch with 1A and 1B in each stitch to add a total of 25A and 25B. *Note:* Continue the established pattern by always stringing the A before the B in each stitch (**fig. 1, red**).

ROUND 5: String 1A and 1B; pass through the next B of Round 4 (this forms the first herringbone stitch). String 1B; pass through nearest A of Round 4. Repeat from the beginning of this round twenty-four times to add a total of 25A and 50B (**fig. 2, blue**).

ROUND 6 (FLOWER TIPS): String 3A, then pass through the next 2B of Round 5 and up through the nearest A of Round 5 to form a picot; repeat twenty-four times to add a total of 75A. Step up through the first 3A added in this round (**fig. 2, red**). Secure the tail thread and trim; don't trim the working thread. *Note:* The picots added in this round form the tips of the flower petals on the outside edge of the ring.

2 **First ring, front.** Fold long loops of beads over the back half of the ring to give the look of circular herringbone stitch, then complete the front with tubular peyote stitch:

ROUND 7 (PETALS): String 7A and pass through the next 3A of Round 6 to form a loop; repeat twenty-four times to add a total of 25 loops with 7A in each. Step up through the first 4A added in this round (**fig. 3**). *Note:* This forms the petals for the front of the ring; once attached to Round 2, they will take on the look of circular herringbone stitch.

ROUND 8: Fold the loops of Round 7 toward the center of the ring, to cover Rounds 1–5. Pass through the nearest H of Round 2 and the middle (fourth) A of the next Round 7 loop (**fig. 4, blue**); repeat around, attaching the tip of each petal to Round 2 (**fig. 4, red**).

ROUND 9: String 1H and pass through the next middle A of Round 7; repeat twenty-four times to add a total of 25H (**fig. 5, purple**). *Note:* Step up for this and each subsequent round by passing through the first bead added in the current round.

ROUND 10: Work tubular peyote stitch with 1B in each stitch to add a total of 25B (**fig. 5, blue**).

ROUND 11: Repeat Round 10 (**fig. 5, red**).

3 **Green ring, center.** Complete the green ring by working a few more rounds of tubular peyote stitch off the back of the ring, then zip the inside edges closed:

SET UP: Weave through beads to exit Round 9, then pass the needle between beads, straight through to the other side of the ring near Round 2. Flip the work over and weave through beads to exit from the left side of a Round 1 bead.

ROUND 12: Work off Round 1 with 1A in each stitch to add a total of 25A (**fig. 6, blue**). *Note:* Step up for this and each subsequent round by passing through the first bead added in the current round.

ROUND 13: Work 1A in each stitch to add a total of 25A (**fig. 6, red**).

ZIP: Fold the center edges toward each other so that Round 13 meets Round 11 and zip the edges together (**fig. 7**, page 146). Secure the thread and trim. Set the green ring aside.

4 **Additional rings.** Create additional rings:

GREEN RINGS: Repeat Steps 1–3 three times for a total of 4 green rings.

PURPLE IRIS RINGS: Repeat Steps 1–3 four times using D in place of B and J in place of H for a total of 4 purple iris rings.

BLUE IRIS RINGS: Repeat Steps 1–3 four times using F in place of B and L in place of H for a total of 4 blue iris rings.

5 **Additional rings and chain.** Join the rings into a chain by linking them with more rings:

FIRST BLUE HEMATITE JOINING RING: Repeat Steps 1–3 using C in place of B and I in place of H, but, before knotting the beads of Rounds 1 and 2 into a circle,

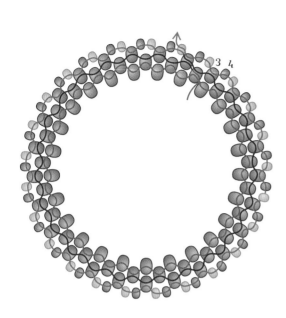

fig. 1: forming rounds 1–4

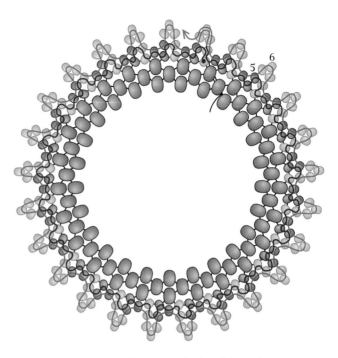

fig. 2: working rounds 5 and 6 on the
back of the ring

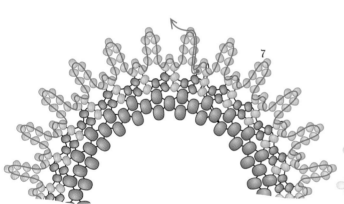

fig. 3: adding round 7

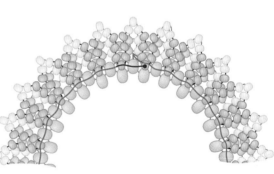

fig. 4: folding down the petals of round 7 and
joining them to round 2 in round 8

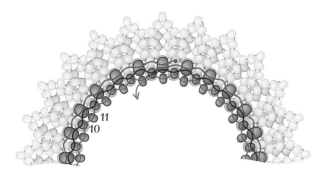

fig. 5: working rounds 9–11 on the front of the ring

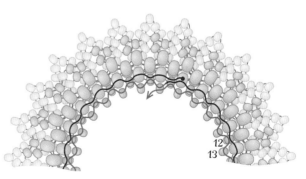

fig. 6: adding rounds 12 and 13 on the
back of the ring

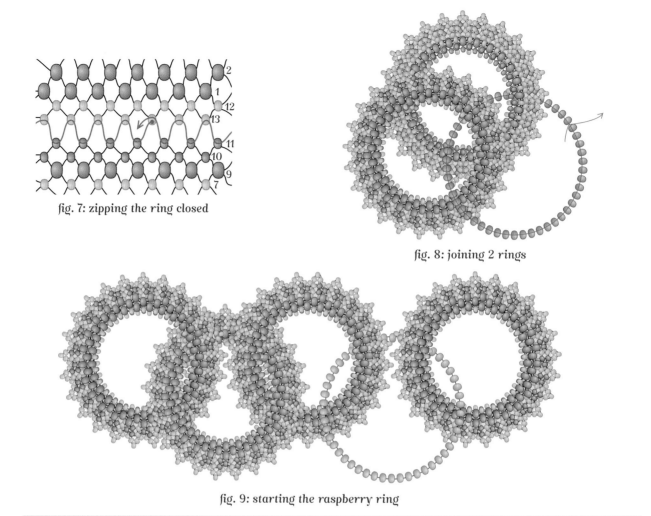

fig. 7: zipping the ring closed

fig. 8: joining 2 rings

fig. 9: starting the raspberry ring

string 1 green ring and 1 purple iris ring. *Note:* When stringing the previous rings and working subsequent rounds, hold the rings so their front faces touch **(fig. 8)**.

FIRST RASPBERRY JOINING RING: Repeat Steps 1–3 using E in place of B and K in place of H, but, before knotting the beads of Rounds 1 and 2 into a circle, string 1 blue iris ring and the previously placed purple iris ring; again, make sure the front faces of the previously beaded rings touch while stringing. *Note:* Before working Round 3, lay the rings flat on your work surface to orient yourself with the direction of the rings. Position the 3 previous rings

so they all lie facedown. As you begin working the back of this new ring, it should overlap the joining rings in the same manner as the blue hematite joining ring **(fig. 9)**. When this ring is complete, like sides should touch when you hold it up against the previous joining ring.

FIRST PURPLE HEMATITE JOINING RING: Repeat Steps 1–3 using G in place of B and M in place of H, but, before knotting the beads of Rounds 1 and 2 into a circle, string 1 new green ring and the previously placed blue iris ring. Again, be sure to pay attention to the orientation of the rings.

Repeat this entire step three times to complete the chain. The final purple hematite ring will connect to only the previous blue iris ring and act at the clasp loop.

6 **Toggle bar.** Use twisted tubular herringbone stitch to form the toggle bar:

ROUND 1: Use 6' (183 cm) of thread to string 6A, leaving a 6" (15 cm) tail. Tie a square knot with the tail and working threads to form a circle. Exit the first bead added, making sure the knot doesn't slip inside the bead **(fig. 10, green)**.

ROUND 2: String 2A and pass through the next 2A of Round 1; repeat twice to add a total of 6A **(fig. 10, blue)**. *Note:* Step up for

this and each subsequent round by passing through the first bead added in the current round.

ROUND 3: Work 3 tubular herringbone stitches with 2A in each stitch to add a total of 6A (**fig. 10, red**).

ROUND 4: String 2A, pass down through the next A of the previous round, and pass up through the following top 2A (A of Round 2 and A of Round 3) in the next column; repeat twice to add a total of 6A (**fig. 11, red; shown as flat side view for clarity**). *Note:* This begins the spiral.

ROUNDS 5–28: Repeat Round 4 twenty-four times.

ROUND 29: String 1A, pass down through the next A of Round 28, and pass up through the following A of Round 28 (**fig. 12, green**); repeat twice to add a total of 3A (**fig. 12, blue**). Pass through the 3A just added twice to reinforce (**fig. 12, red**). Weave through beads to exit from 1A of Round 13. Set the thread aside.

ROUND 30: Insert two 1⅛" (2.8 cm) pieces of wire into the open end of the toggle bar. Add a needle to the tail thread and repeat Round 29 to close the end of the tube and enclose the wires. Secure the tail thread and trim; don't trim the working thread.

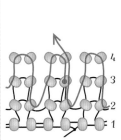

fig. 10: working rounds 1–3 of the toggle bar

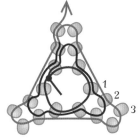

fig. 11: starting the spiral of round 4

fig. 12: closing the end of the toggle bar

147

7 Toggle band. Use tubular peyote stitch to form a band around the toggle bar:

ROUNDS 1 AND 2: Use the working thread to string 16G. Wrap the strand of beads around the toggle bar and pass through the beads again to form a circle **(fig. 13, pink)**.

ROUND 3: String 1G, skip 1G previously strung, and pass through the next G; repeat seven times to add a total of 8G **(fig. 13, purple)**. *Note:* Step up for this and each subsequent round by passing through the first bead added in the current round.

ROUND 4: Work 1A in each stitch to add a total of 8A. Weave through beads to exit 1G of Round 1 **(fig. 13, green)**.

ROUNDS 5 AND 6: Work 1G in each stitch to add a total of 8G in each of 2 rounds **(fig. 13, blue)**.

ROUND 7: Work 1A in each stitch to add a total of 8A **(fig. 13, red)**. Weave through beads to exit 1G of Round 1.

EMBELLISHMENT: String the crystal flower and 1A; pass back through the flower and through the last G exited in Round 1 **(fig. 14, blue)**. Repeat the thread path to reinforce.

ASSEMBLY: Weave through beads to exit 1A of Round 4 on the side opposite the flower. String 2A, 1M, and 2A; pass through the middle A of the ring's Round 6 picot on the first ring. String 2A; pass through the middle A of the next Round 6 picot on the same ring. String 2A; pass back through the M just added. String 2A; pass through 1A of Round 7, across from the last A exited on the band **(fig. 14, red)**. Weave through beads to repeat the thread path to reinforce. Secure the thread and trim.

TIPS

- Additional length can be added to the chain by simply beading more rings. Each 1½" (3.8 cm) link will add ¾" (2 cm) to the necklace length due to overlapping.

- In lieu of an entire necklace of beaded chain, you can extend the length with other elements such as seed-beaded components, chain, ribbon, beaded rope, or kumihimo cord.

- You can also use the individual rings as components. By varying the number of beads used for Rounds 1 and 2, you can create graduated rings. Be sure to start with an even number of beads. Starting with fewer than 30 beads will make the ring hard to finish and zip together. Also note that in order to create the linked chain, the inner opening of each ring will need to accommodate 2 rings.

- As the necklace is worn, the rings may become oval in shape. Reshape the rings with your fingers as needed.

- The components in this design can also be easily converted to earrings. Or instead of zipping the two sides together, experiment with encapsulating a rhinestone or rivoli in the center of a component by bezeling it with more rounds of peyote stitch on the inside edges.

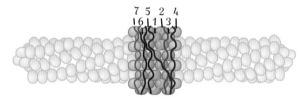

fig. 13: forming the toggle band

fig. 14: adding the embellishment and connecting the toggle

DESIGN OPTIONS

BY LISA KAN

- The flexibility and versatility of this design is that it can be worn in three ways: Wear with all of the rings faceup (as shown in the bronze main project), turn the necklace around to show off the backs of the rings (shown above), or mix it up by flipping over every other ring (shown at left).

- Longer lengths of this necklace are also beautiful. The two variations shown at right—in a pretty mixed-purple colorway and a blend of dark, lime, aqua, and teal shades of green—are each made with 30 rings, resulting in necklaces 22½" (57.2 cm) long.

A combination of size 8° and size 11° seed beads creates perfect curves in this bracelet's paisley-shaped components. The peacock color palette features shades of green, gray, and purple seed beads paired with bronze pressed-glass rondelles.
● *by Melinda Barta*

paisley paillettes

TECHNIQUES
Tubular herringbone stitch

Ladder stitch and quick-start ladder stitch variation

Square stitch

Fringe

Stitch-in-the-ditch embellishment

MATERIALS
1 g metallic bronze size 15° Japanese seed beads (A)

0.5 g metallic plum hematite size 15° Japanese seed beads

0.5 g metallic cabernet iris size 15° Japanese seed beads

2 g matte metallic olive-gold size 11° seed beads (B)

2 g matte metallic sage gray iris size 11° seed beads

1 g matte metallic cabernet iris size 11° seed beads

2 g matte metallic red-purple iris size 11° seed beads

4 g matte metallic olive-gold size 8° seed beads (C)

4 g matte metallic sage gray iris size 8° seed beads

4 g matte metallic cabernet iris size 8° seed beads

4 g matte metallic red-purple iris size 8° seed beads

13 light topaz Picasso 4×3mm pressed-glass faceted rondelles

10 metallic dark bronze 8×5mm pressed-glass faceted rondelles

1½" (3.8 cm) of sterling silver 24-gauge wire

Purple and tan One-G nylon beading thread

Smoke 6 lb braided beading thread

TOOLS
Scissors

Size 10 and 12 beading needles

FINISHED SIZE
6⅞" (17.2 cm)

NOTE
Start with the size 10 needle and switch to the size 12 if you ever have trouble fitting the needle through beads.

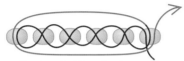

fig. 1: stitching the base ring

fig. 2: joining the center beads of the base ring to form a 3×2 grid

fig. 3: working round 1

fig. 4: stitching round 2

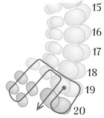

fig. 5: adding 2C and 4B in round 20

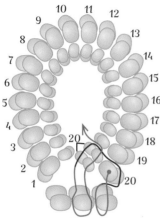

fig. 6: connecting the rope to the base ring

1 Paisley base. Use ladder, square, and tubular herringbone stitches to form the curved base of a paisley:

BASE RING: Use 7' (213 cm) of tan thread and the quick-start ladder stitch variation (page 22) to form a strip 6C long, leaving a 6" (15 cm) tail **(fig. 1, blue)**. Stitch the first and last C together to form a ring **(fig. 1, red)**. Fold the ring in half and use square stitch to join the 2 center C **(fig. 2, blue)**. Exit up through an end C **(fig. 2, red)**. *Note:* This forms a 3-bead-wide and 2-bead-deep grid.

ROUND 1: String 2C; pass down through the next end C and up through the nearest center C **(fig. 3, blue)**. String 2B; pass down through the other center C and up through the first end C exited. Step up through the first C added in this round **(fig. 3, red)**.

ROUND 2: String 2C; pass down through the next C and up through the nearest B of the previous round. String 2B; pass down through the next B and up through the nearest C of the previous round. *Note:* Step up for this and each subsequent round by passing through the first bead added in the current round **(fig. 4)**.

ROUNDS 3–19: Repeat Round 2 seventeen times, using tight tension to encourage the rope to curve toward the other end of the base ring. Secure and trim the tail thread.

ROUND 20: Repeat Round 2, this time stringing 4B instead of 2B **(fig. 5)**.

CONNECT: Connect the end of the rope to the other end of the base ring following a tubular herringbone thread path without adding any beads: Making sure the rope isn't twisted, fold it down toward the other end of the ring base. Pass down through the nearest end C and up though the next end C **(fig. 6, green)**. Pass through the next C of Round 20 and the following 2B of Round 20 **(fig. 6, blue)**. Pass down through the nearest center C of the base ring. Pass up through the other center C of the base ring and through the next 2B of Round 20 **(fig. 6, red)**.

2 Paisley tip. Use ladder, square, and tubular herring-bone stitches to form the tip of a paisley:

ROUND 21: Rotate the work 180° and weave through beads to exit the bottom left end C of the base ring. String 2C; pass down through the next end C and up through the nearest center C **(fig. 7, green)**. Weave through beads to exit up through an end C on the other end of the base ring **(fig. 7, blue)**. Square-stitch 2C to the 2 end C of the ring base and step up through the first C just added **(fig. 7, red)**.

ROUND 22: Working counterclockwise (when looking down at the base ring), work tubular herringbone stitch with 2C in each stitch. Step up through the first C added in this round **(fig. 8)**. Join all of the beads of this round with a ladder-stitch thread path. Exit away from the work **(fig. 9, blue and red)**.

3 Embellishment. Add a rondelle to the center of the paisley, a fringe at the tip, and accent beads along the outside edge:

CENTER RONDELLE: Rotate the work 180° and weave through beads to exit 1C on the outside edge of the paisley, between Rounds 5 and 6. Pass between the adjacent B toward the center of the paisley. String 1 bronze rondelle; pass between the B and C directly across from those just exited. *Note:* You'll most likely exit between Rounds 15 and 16, but slightly adjust the angle of the needle if needed to snug the bronze rondelle in the top curve of the paisley. Pass down through the nearest C of Round 16 and C of Round 17, then pass up through the next C of Round 17 and C of Round 16. Pass back

through the rope between the inside B and through the bronze rondelle (**fig. 10, blue**). Pass between the inside B to exit the outside edge. Pass up through the nearest C of Round 6 and C of Round 7, then down through the next C of Round 7 and C of Round 6 (**fig. 10, red**). Repeat the entire thread path to reinforce. *Note:* Make sure your turnarounds on the outside edge of the paisley match the herringbone thread path; this is why the blue-colored stitch goes down and the red-colored stitch goes up in **fig. 10**.

FRINGE: Rotate the work 180° and weave through beads to exit 1C of Round 22. String

fig. 7: working round 21 off of the bottom of the base ring

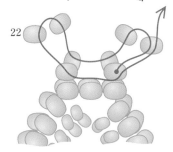

fig. 8: adding round 22

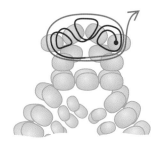

fig. 9: ladder-stitching the beads of round 22

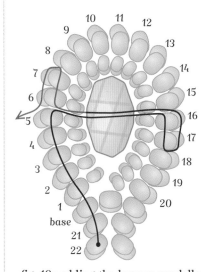

fig. 10: adding the bronze rondelle

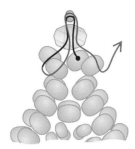

fig. 11: forming the fringe

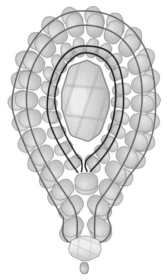

fig. 12: reinforcing the columns

fig. 13: adding the edge accents
along the outside of the paisley

fig. 14: forming a fringe at the end
of the toggle bar

1 topaz rondelle and 1A; pass back through the topaz rondelle and the next C of Round 22 (**fig. 11, blue**). Pass up through the following C of Round 22 and weave through beads to exit the next C of Round 22, using tight tension to center the fringe over the tip of the paisley (**fig. 11, red**).

REINFORCE: Weave through the columns of B to reinforce (**fig. 12, blue**). Weave through the columns of C to reinforce (**fig. 12, red**).

EDGE ACCENTS: Exit from 1C of Round 22, away from the topaz rondelle and on the outside edge of the paisley. String 1A and pass up through the C diagonally across from the C just exited; repeat along the outside edge of the paisley to add a total of 25A stitch-in-the-ditch embellishments (**fig. 13**). Set aside; don't trim the working thread.

4 Remaining paisleys. Make additional paisleys in the following colorways:

GREEN PAISLEYS: Repeat Steps 1–3 for a total of 2 green paisleys. Repeat again, omitting the topaz rondelle fringe; the toggle bar will attach to the end of this paisley.

GRAY PAISLEYS: Repeat Steps 1–3 twice using smoke thread, gray 11°s in place of B and gray 8°s in place of C for a total of 2 gray paisleys. Repeat again, omitting the bronze rondelle; this will be used as the clasp loop.

CABERNET PAISLEYS: Repeat Steps 1–3 twice using purple thread, cabernet 15°s in place of A for the edge accents, cabernet 11°s in place of B, and cabernet 8°s in place of C for a total of 2 cabernet paisleys.

RED-PURPLE PAISLEYS: Repeat Steps 1–3 three times using purple thread, plum 15°s in place of A for the edge accents, red-purple 11°s in place of B, and red-purple 8°s in place of C for a total of 3 red-purple paisleys.

5 Toggle bar. Use tubular herringbone stitch to form a toggle bar, using cabernet size 11°s unless otherwise noted:

TUBE ROUND 1: Use 4' (122 cm) of new purple thread to ladder-stitch 4 beads, leaving a 12" (30.5 cm) tail. Ladder-stitch the first and last beads to form a ring.

TUBE ROUNDS 2–12: String 2 beads, then pass down through the next bead of the previous round and up through the following bead of the previous round; repeat. Step up for this and each subsequent round by passing through the first bead of the current round. Continue in tubular herringbone stitch for a total of 12 rounds. Stitch through the last round of beads following a ladder-stitch thread path. Exit away from the beadwork from 1 end bead.

FIRST END: String 1 topaz rondelle and 1 cabernet 15°; pass back through the rondelle and the bead of Round 12 opposite the last one exited and up through the next bead of Round 12 (**fig. 14**). Repeat the thread path to center the topaz rondelle over the end of the tube and connecting to all end beads of Round 12. Weave through beads to exit 7 beads from the end of the tube, toward the center; don't trim the thread.

WIRE: Insert two ¾" (2 cm) pieces of wire inside the tube and hold them in place while finishing the ends. *Note:* It's okay if you can only fit 1 wire inside the tube.

SECOND END: Add a needle to the tail thread and finish the opposite end of the tube as you did for the first end. Secure the tail thread and trim.

CONNECTION: Use the working thread to string 1 cabernet size 11° and 1 topaz rondelle; pass through beads in Rounds 22 and 21 at the tip of the green paisley without a fringe from Step 4. Pass back through the topaz rondelle and the 7 beads just strung and up through the next bead of the toggle bar (**fig. 15**). Weave through beads to exit one of the beads marked with a blue X in **fig. 15** and repeat the thread path through the connection, centering the topaz rondelle over the tip of the green paisley. When attaching to the toggle bar on the return, pass through the bead marked with a blue X in **fig. 15** not previously entered.

EDGE ACCENTS: Following the same technique for the edge accents in Step 3, add A along the two sides of the toggle bar closest to the connection. Secure the thread and trim.

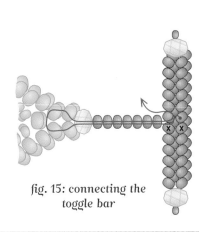

fig. 15: connecting the toggle bar

6 Assembly: Use square stitch to join the paisleys:

JOIN: Lay out the paisleys according to **fig. 16** and weave the remaining working threads through beads to square-stitch the connecting beads marked in red. *Note:* Work 1–3 square stitches at each connection (**fig. 16**). Only connect the bottom C touching the work surface (**fig. 17**); leaving the top C unconnected allows the bracelet to curve around your wrist and makes the edge accents more noticeable. Secure the threads and trim.

TIPS

- When herringbone-stitching with beads as large as size 8°, it's especially important to have your thread match your beads because the long thread float from one bead to the next remains exposed.

- The gray paisley makes a great clasp loop because the smoke braided beading thread makes it stiffer than the paisleys worked with nylon thread.

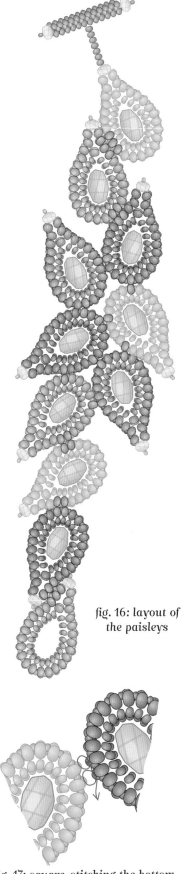

fig. 16: layout of the paisleys

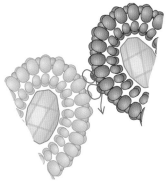

fig. 17: square-stitching the bottom edge of 2 paisleys

DESIGN OPTION

Semiprecious Paisley Necklace

BY MELINDA BARTA

Bead a striking focal piece with 5 paisleys side by side and then add straps of labradorite and garnet stones. Each paisley center is adorned with labradorite ovals and rondelles to coordinate with the beads on the straps.

MATERIALS

0.5 g metallic cabernet iris size 15° Japanese seed beads

1 g matte metallic sage gray iris size 11° seed beads

0.5 g matte metallic cabernet iris size 11° seed beads

1 g matte metallic red-purple iris size 11° seed beads

2 g matte metallic sage gray iris size 8° seed beads

1 g matte metallic cabernet iris size 8° seed beads

2 g matte metallic red-purple iris size 8° seed beads

36 garnet 3×2mm faceted rondelles

25 labradorite 4×2mm faceted rondelles

5 labradorite 5mm faceted rounds

24 labradorite 6mm faceted rounds

15 labradorite 6×8mm faceted oval coins

4 sterling silver 2mm crimp tubes

4 sterling silver 3mm crimp covers

1 sterling silver 9×23mm box clasp with labradorite inlay

20" (51 cm) of fine (.014") 21-strand stainless steel beading wire

Purple One-G nylon beading thread

Smoke 6 lb braided beading thread

TOOLS

Scissors

Size 10 and 13 beading needles

Wire cutters

Crimping pliers

FINISHED SIZE

18" (45.5 cm)

1 PAISLEY BASE AND TIP.
Repeat Steps 1 and 2 of Paisley Paillettes (page 152) using braided beading thread, matte metallic sage gray iris size 11°s for B, and matte metallic sage gray iris size 8° seed beads for C.

Note: Use the size 10 needle when stitching the size 8°s and 11°s of the paisley; use the 13 needle when stitching the stones.

2 EMBELLISHMENT.
Repeat Step 3 of Paisley Paillettes, adding 1 labradorite rondelle and 1 labradorite oval at the center of the paisley. When adding these center beads, string the rondelle before the oval and stitch from the base ring toward the top edge of the paisley base, not horizontally across the paisley as you did with the bronze rondelles for Paisley Paillettes. For the fringe, add one 5mm round and 1 metallic cabernet iris size 15°. Skip the edge accents step.

3 REMAINING PAISLEYS.
Repeat Steps 1 and 2 for a second gray paisley. Repeat Steps 1 and 2 twice using purple thread and matte metallic red-purple iris size 11° and 8°s. Repeat Steps 1 and 2 using purple thread and matte metallic cabernet iris size 11°s and 8°s; for the fringe, use one 5mm round, 1 rondelle, and 1 metallic cabernet iris size 15°.

4 FOCAL ASSEMBLY.
Arrange the paisleys in a V shape with the cabernet iris paisley at the center and the gray paisleys on the ends. In the sample shown here, the red-purple paisleys are stitched to each other in the center of the necklace, as well as to the cabernet iris paisley. Use square stitches to join the paisleys as in Step 6 of Paisley Paillettes, but this time join the top and bottom herringbone beads that touch along the sides.

5 STRAPS.
Use 10" (25.5 cm) of beading wire to string 1 crimp tube. Pass through 1 bead on the outside edge of 1 gray paisley, passing through the bead that will allow the focal to hang as desired. Pass back through the crimp tube and crimp. *String 1 garnet, 1 rondelle, 1 oval, and 1 rondelle. String {1 garnet and one 6mm round} three times. Repeat from * three times. String 1 rondelle, 1 oval, 1 rondelle, 1 garnet, 1 crimp tube, and one half of the clasp; pass back through the tube and crimp.

Repeat this entire step on the other side of the focal, connecting to the outside edge of the other gray paisley and using the other half of the clasp. Cover each crimp tube with a crimp cover. *Note:* The crimp covers used here were oxidized to coordinate with the labradorite; see page 95 for oxidizing how-to.

beyond the basics

ADDITIONAL BEADWEAVING STITCHES

It's common to see designs that combine herringbone with other stitches, and many of the projects in this book are no exception. Here are some of the most common techniques you'll encounter. See the Finishing Touches technique section (page 133) for detailed information on how to transition from herringbone to many of these stitches and vice versa.

square stitch

Begin by stringing all the beads for Row 1. For Row 2, string 1 bead, pass through the last bead of Row 1, and through the bead just strung **(fig. 1, blue)**. Add 1 bead to each bead of the previous row by stringing 1 bead, passing through the next bead of the previous row, and through the bead just strung **(fig. 1, red)**. Stitch the following rows in the same manner.

You don't always have to start square stitch with a strand of beads. To form a 2-bead-wide **square-stitch strip** off of an edge of beadwork, string 2 beads, then pass through the last 2 beads exited and up through the first bead strung **(fig. 2, blue)**. String 2 beads, then pass down through the second bead of the previous row and up through the first bead of the previous row and the first bead just added; repeat for the length of the strip **(fig. 2, red)**. You may hear other designers call this 2-bead or single-column herringbone stitch.

See Spiraling Narrow Band on page 105 for how to make this strip spiral.

peyote stitch

For **flat even-count peyote stitch**, string an even number of beads to create the first 2 rows **(fig. 3, blue)**. *Note:* This first set of beads make up both Row 1 and Row 2. To work the first stitch of Row 3, string

1 bead and pass back through the second-to-last bead of the previous row. To continue across the row, string 1 bead, skip the next bead of the starting strand, and pass back through the next. Continue adding 1 bead at a time, passing over every other bead of the previous row **(fig. 3, red)**.

Think of this peyote mantra as you bead: "String 1 bead, skip 1 bead, and pass through the next." Snug the beads at the end of the row and work the following rows in the same manner.

Because there is 1 bead in each stitch, this is called **one-drop** peyote stitch; for **two-drop**, work 2 beads in each stitch as if they were 1.

Begin a **mid-row/mid-round increase** by working 1 stitch with 2 beads in 1 row **(fig. 4, blue)**. In the next row, work 1 bead in each stitch, adding 1 bead between the pair added in the previous row **(fig. 4, red)**. This is referred to as "splitting the pair." For a smooth increase, use very narrow beads for both the pair of beads added in the first increase row/round and the bead that splits the pair in the following round.

To form a **mid-row/mid-round decrease**, simply pass the thread through the next 2 beads of the previous row/round without adding a bead **(fig. 5, blue)**. In the next row/round, work 1 bead in each stitch as usual, placing 1 bead over the decrease **(fig. 5, red)**. Work with tight tension to avoid holes.

For **flat odd-count peyote**, begin by stringing an odd number of beads for Rows 1 and 2. For Row 3, string 1 bead, skip the last bead strung, and pass back through the next bead; repeat across the row. To add the last bead, string 1 bead, snug the beads, and knot the tail and working

fig. 1

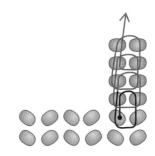

fig. 2

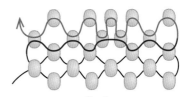

fig. 3

fig. 4

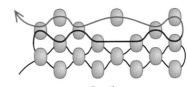

fig. 5

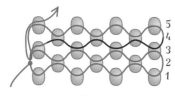

fig. 6

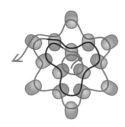

fig. 7

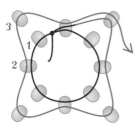

fig. 8

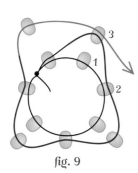

fig. 9

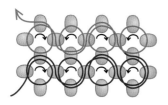

fig. 10

threads. Step up for Row 4 by passing back through the last bead added (**fig. 6, green**). Continue in peyote stitch, turning as for even-count at the end of this and all even-numbered rows (**fig. 6, blue**). At the end of all odd-numbered rows, string 1 bead, pass under the thread loop at the edge of the previous row, and pass back through the last bead added (**fig. 6, red**).

For Round 1 of **circular peyote stitch**, string 3 beads and knot the tail and working threads to form a circle; pass through the first bead strung (**fig. 7, green**). For Round 2, string 2 beads and pass through the next bead of the previous round; repeat twice (**fig. 7, blue**). Step up by passing through the first bead of the current round. For Round 3, string 1 bead and pass through the next bead of the previous round; repeat around and step up as before (**fig. 7, red**). Continue in this manner, alternating Rounds 2 and 3, adjusting the bead count as necessary to keep the work flat.

For **even-count tubular peyote stitch,** string an even number of beads and tie a square knot to form a circle. This starting circle forms Rounds 1 and 2. Pass through the first bead strung (**fig. 8, blue**). For Round 3, string 1 bead, skip 1 bead, and pass through the next bead; repeat around, following the peyote mantra, until you have added half the number of beads of the first round. Step up through the first bead added in this round (**fig. 8, red**). For each of the following rounds, work 1 bead in each stitch and continue to step up at the end of each round.

For **odd-count tubular peyote stitch,** form the starting circle with an odd number of beads. Pass through the first bead strung. For Round 3, work 1 bead in each stitch following the peyote mantra.

After you work your way around the starting circle (**fig. 9, blue**), string 1 bead and pass through the first bead added in this round (**fig. 9, red**). Pull the beadwork so the Round 3 beads stack on top of the Round 1 beads. Continue working 1 bead in each stitch for the desired length; no step ups are needed.

For more basic information on peyote, plus advanced techniques and variations, refer to *Mastering Peyote Stitch* (Interweave, 2012).

right-angle weave

For **flat right-angle weave,** string 4 beads and pass through the first 3 beads again to form the first unit of Row 1. For each of the following units in this row, string 3 beads, then pass through the last bead exited in the previous unit and the first 2 beads just strung. The thread path will resemble a series of figure eights, alternating directions with each unit. To set up for the next row, exit toward the work from the top bead of the final unit (**fig. 10, blue**). For Unit 1 of Row 2, string 3 beads, then pass through the last bead exited and the first bead just strung. *For Unit 2, string 2 beads, then pass back through the next top bead of the previous row, the last bead exited in the previous unit, and the 2 beads just strung. For Unit 3, pass through the next top bead of the previous row, string 2 beads, then pass through the last bead of the previous unit in this row, the top bead just exited, and the first bead just strung. Repeat from * to complete the row, then step up for a new row as before (**fig. 10, red**).

When working **tubular right-angle weave,** turn Row 1 into a circle by connecting the end bead of the second-to-last unit to the end bead of the first unit while beading the final unit (**fig. 11**). For the next and subsequent rounds, work right-angle weave off the top beads of the previous round as when working flat right-angle weave; continue to close each round by joining the first and second-to-last units as before.

picot

A **picot** is a decorative net, most often made with 3 beads, used to embellish a beadwork surface

(fig. 12). See more embellishment techniques starting on page 133.

brick stitch

See page 57 for how to use brick stitch as a base for circular herringbone. On page 135, you'll discover how it's the ideal stitch to use for the starting row/round of bead embroidery.

fig. 11

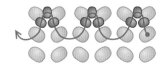

fig. 12

CRIMPING, WIREWORKING, AND KNOTTING

crimping

This is a technique by which you mold a crimp tube or bead around beading wire using crimping or flat-nose pliers. Most often this technique is used to attach a clasp to a piece of jewelry, thereby creating a secure finish.

Crimp tubes: Use beading wire to string 1 crimp tube, pass through a finding, and pass back through the tube, leaving a ¼" to ½" (6 mm to 1.3 cm) tail.

Make sure the wires do not cross inside the tube. Pinch the tube into a U shape, using the back notch of the crimping pliers. Each wire should now be contained in its own chamber.

Turn the pinched tube 90° and use the front notch of the crimping pliers to fold it into a cylinder. Trim the excess wire **(fig. 13)**.

Crimp covers: Hold the cover in the front notch of the crimping pliers, position it over a crimped crimp tube, and gently squeeze the pliers to form the C-shaped finding into a round bead. For a perfectly round crimp cover, rotate the pliers around the cover just before you pinch the cover completely closed **(fig. 14)**.

basic wirework

Jump rings: Using two pairs of chain- or flat-nose pliers (round-nose pliers usually leave marks) or a combination of the two, open and close a jump ring by twisting the sides in opposite directions, one side straight toward you and one side straight away from you (pulling the ends away from each other will distort the rings). To close the jump ring, reverse this action **(fig. 15)**.

A **simple loop** can be opened and closed like a jump ring, so if you want to change its placement, you can do so easily. Because there is a small opening in the loop, beware that a beading thread could slip through.

Use chain- or flat-nose pliers to form a 90° bend ½" to 1" (1.3 to 2.5 cm) from the end of your wire **(fig. 16)**. Imagine the size of the loop you would like to make, then place the nose of the round-nose pliers on the short wire at a distance from the bend that equals about half of the circumference of the loop you imagined. Roll the pliers toward the bend, then use your finger to wrap the short wire the rest of the way round the pliers, adjusting the pliers as needed, until the short wire crosses the bend at the base of the loop **(fig. 17)**.

fig. 13

fig. 14

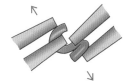

fig. 15

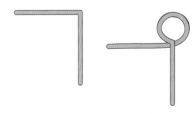

fig. 16   *fig. 17*

While still holding the loop in the pliers, adjust the wire below the bend as needed to restore the 90° angle. Trim the wire next to the bend **(fig. 18)**.

A **wrapped loop** is a sturdy loop that is preferable when creating a dangle or link that is heavy or will incur strain. Because it can't open like a simple loop once complete, it's safe to attach beading thread to this type of loop. To begin, use chain- or flat-nose pliers to form a 90° bend 1" to 2" (2.5 to 5 cm) from the end of your wire.

Make a simple loop, but don't trim the tail. Grasp the loop with chain-nose pliers. Using your fingers, or holding the end of the wire with chain- or flat-nose pliers, wrap the tail down the neck of the main wire at the base of the loop for about 2 or 3 wraps. Trim the wire at the end of the last wrap. For tight wraps, think of pulling the wire away from the loop as you wrap.

Once you've trimmed the wire after making wraps, press the cut end down with either flat-nose pliers or the front notch of crimping pliers **(fig. 19)**.

Wrapped-loop dangle: Use a head pin to string 1 or more beads and form a wrapped loop **(fig. 20)**.

knotting

An **overhand knot** is the most basic knot. Make a loop with your stringing material by crossing the left end over the right. Pass the left end through the loop from the back so that it resembles a pretzel. Pull the thread tight **(fig. 21)**.

Use a **square knot** when securing a starting circle of beads. Begin by tying an overhand knot: Cross the working thread **(fig. 22, red)** over the tail thread **(fig. 22, blue)** and pass the tail thread through the loop from front to back. Make a second overhand knot, passing the tail thread **(fig. 23, blue)** behind the working thread **(fig. 23, red)** and through the loop just formed from front to back. Pull the threads tight, making sure the knot is between the first and last beads of the circle. Before beginning the next round, pass the working thread through the first or last bead strung to correctly orient the thread, but don't pull so tight that the knot gets pulled inside the bead. If the knot slips inside the bead and fills the hole with thread, you'll have less room for your needle on subsequent passes. Forcing your needle through small spaces can cause bead breakage.

To form a **slipknot,** fold your thread in your hand so the tail forms the top half of the fold. Grab the top 1" (2.5 cm) of the fold and flip it up away from you to form the first loop, with the working thread crossed on top of the tail thread **(fig. 24; tail thread is blue, working thread is red)**. Reach through the loop from back to front, grasp the tail thread just below the cross (not the end of the tail itself), and pull the tail thread through the loop, forming a second loop **(fig. 25)**. Slowly pull on the threads to tighten the first loop around the tail thread and to adjust the size of the larger second loop.

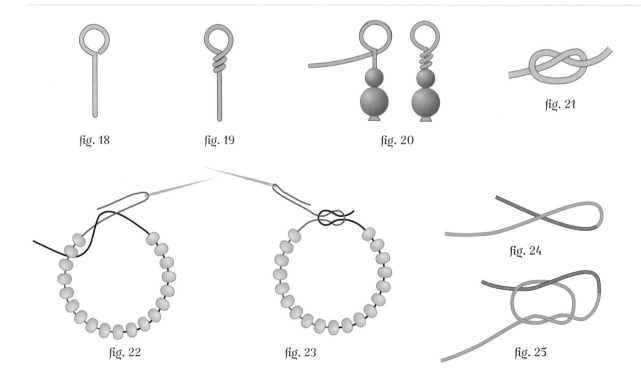

fig. 18   fig. 19   fig. 20   fig. 21

fig. 22   fig. 23   fig. 24   fig. 25

CONTRIBUTORS

about the author

MELINDA BARTA is editor of *Beadwork* magazine. When she's not beading, Melinda loves spending time with her family in the Colorado outdoors. She is the author of four other books—including *Mastering Peyote Stitch* (Interweave, 2012) and *Custom Cool Jewelry* (Interweave, 2008)—and has filmed many instructional DVDs on beadweaving techniques. Melinda has taught her craft at Penland School of Crafts, at John C. Campbell Folk School, and at bead shows across the country; she has assisted workshops at Haystack Mountain School and Arrowmont School of Craft. Melinda has shared her love of beading, embroidery, and teaching on DIY, PBS, HGTV, Style, and local television networks. See her "Custom Cool" column in each issue of *Beadwork*. Visit melindabarta.com.

contributing designers

JEAN CAMPBELL writes about, teaches, and designs beadwork. She has written and edited more than forty-five books, most recently including *Steampunk Style Jewelry* and *Creating Glamorous Jewelry with Swarovski Elements* (both Creative Publishing International, 2010). Jean is a Create Your Style Crystallized Elements Ambassador for the Swarovski Company and contributes to BeadingDaily.com. She is the senior editor of *Beadwork* magazine and conducts lectures and teaches jewelry-making workshops throughout the United States. Jean was a *Beadwork* magazine Designer of the Year in 2009. Visit jeancampbellink.blogspot.com.

LESLIE FRAZIER has been designing jewelry and teaching beadwork classes throughout the United States, Japan, Canada, and Colombia since 1996. Many of her designs combine several stitches, and she has developed many innovative techniques that she loves to share with her students. Her designs were among those featured in *Beadweaving: Major Works by Leading Artists, Showcase 500: Beaded Jewelry, The Art & Elegance of Beadweaving*, and *I Can Herringbone* (all Lark, 2008–2012), as well as several Japanese publications. She was a *Beadwork* magazine Designer of the Year in 2012. Visit Leslie on Facebook and at lesliefrazier.com.

LISA KAN is a beadweaver, jewelry designer, and glass artist. With an eye for color and textural balance, Lisa combines basic beading stitches with crystals, pearls, and seed beads to create designs imbued with dimension and depth. Her focus is on wearable, multipurpose, and modular component beadwork design. She developed Aria Design Studio, a line of metal components that are designed to be combined with beadwork. She is the author of *Bead Romantique: Elegant Beadweaving Designs* (Interweave, 2008). Lisa was a *Beadwork* magazine Designer of the Year in 2009. Visit lisakan.com.

CAROLE OHL is a graphic designer by trade who also owns a consignment bead store, called Bead Stash, in Dayton, Ohio. She has practiced many art forms, and so far, beadweaving has "stuck" the longest. Her favorite part of beading is teaching, sharing, and watching people inspire each other with this art form. She is also a certified Zentangle instructor, which she says has only made her a better beader. Carole was a *Beadwork* magazine Designer of the Year in 2010. Visit beadstash.blogspot.com and openseedarts.blogspot.com.

JEAN POWER is an award-winning jewelry designer, teacher, and author of several beadweaving books. Her beadwork is often inspired by the beads and techniques she uses, resulting in a pared-down look with little embellishment but big impact. Jean has been beading for more than ten years, and her love of geometric motifs was sparked with her very first peyote project. In her contribution to this book, Jean combined her love of crystals, cylinder beads, angles, structure, and interchangeable jewelry. When she's not beading, Jean is writing about beading, teaching, buying beads, or competing in roller derby. She was a *Beadwork* magazine Designer of the Year in 2012. Visit jeanpower.com.

KELLY WIESE has been designing beadwork for about sixteen years. She teaches nationally at various bead shows and other venues. Kelly spends as much time as possible working on new designs and keeping up with her online business, Bead Parlor. She is the author of two bead-weaving books, *Beaded Allure* (North Light Books, 2010) and *A Beaded Romance* (David & Charles, 2013). Her three cats and three dogs keep her company in her home studio in Fort Morgan, Colorado. Kelly was a *Beadwork* magazine Designer of the Year in 2011. Visit beadparlor.com.

JILL WISEMAN fell in love with beading in 2001 and now works full time as a national beading teacher. She is the author of *Jill Wiseman's Beautiful Beaded Ropes* (Lark, 2012). Jill is known for writing clear and detailed instructions for all experience levels, and her kits and patterns are sold through her company, Tapestry Beads. She was a *Beadwork* magazine Designer of the Year in 2013. Contact Jill at jill@tapestrybeads.com. Visit tapestrybeads.com.

PROJECT RESOURCES

Check your local bead shop for the materials used in this book or contact the companies listed here (see page 166 for contact information). Remember, some beads and findings may be limited in availability; if the companies don't have the exact beads shown in this book, they will probably have something that will work just as well. Visit melindabarta.com for a list of bead colors and their numbers used in many of the projects.

Reflections and Timeless Cuff

BY MELINDA BARTA (PAGE 32)

Antique copper size 8°s: The Bead Cache. FireLine braided beading thread, Toho sharp triangles, and all other seed beads: Beyond Beadery. Pressed-glass and fire-polished beads: Starman. Wire: FusionBeads.com. Gold-plated clasp: The Whole Bead Shop.

Chiffon Ribbon Cuff and Filigree Square Bracelet

BY CAROLE OHL (PAGE 40)
FILIGREE SQUARE BRACELET BY MELINDA BARTA

Toho triangles and gold beads: Charlene's Beads. Swarovski bicones: INM Crystal. Elegant Elements Clasp: The BeadSmith. Brass filigree square and caps: Kabela Design. Burgundy seed beads, Miyuki cubes, and FireLine braided beading thread: Beyond Beadery. Bugle beads: FusionBeads.com. Antique copper size 8°s: The Bead Cache.

Jeanne Moreau and Design Option

BY JEAN CAMPBELL (PAGE 46)

Seed beads, FireLine braided beading thread, and Swarovski pearls, rounds, and pendant (article #4127): Beyond Beadery. Swarovski pendant also from: FusionBeads.com.

Graceful Garland and Rose Garden Necklace

BY MELINDA BARTA (PAGE 58)

Seed beads, FireLine braided beading thread, and Ultrasuede: Beyond Beadery. Pressed-glass and fire-polished rounds: Starman. Snaps: Jo-Ann Fabric and Craft Stores. Rectangle dangles: The Beadin' Path. Jump rings: Ornamentea. Vintaj chain and swirl clasp: FusionBeads.com or Vintaj Natural Brass Co.

Starbright Bracelet and Design Options
BY KELLY WIESE (PAGE 64)

Nymo nylon beading thread, seed beads, and Swarovski bicones: Beyond Beadery. Swarovski chaton (article #1028): Artbeads.com. Kits: Bead Parlor.

Gilded Blossoms and Chocolate Flower Earrings
BY MELINDA BARTA (PAGE 70)

Chain: Primitive Earth Beads & Chain. Delica cylinder beads, FireLine braided beading thread, and One-G nylon beading thread: Beyond Beadery. Delica cylinder beads also from: FusionBeads.com. Size 8° seed beads: The Bead Cache. Jump rings and clasp: The Whole Bead Shop. Head pins: Rishashay. Vintaj brass ear wires: FusionBeads.com or Vintaj Natural Brass Co. Smoky quartz teardrops: Beaux Beads. Charlottes: Applegate Lapidary.

Tambourine Bangles and Design Options
BY MELINDA BARTA (PAGE 84)

Seed beads and FireLine braided beading thread: Beyond Beadery. Indonesian discs: Bead World.

Hawthorne Necklace
BY MELINDA BARTA (PAGE 90)

Charlottes: Applegate Lapidary. Size 11° Czech seed beads: Applegate Lapidary and A Grain of Sand. Dark blue leather cord (sold as Natural Pacific): Leather Cord USA. Zinc rounds: Knot Just Beads. Lampwork beads: Terri Caspary Schmidt. Wire and FireLine braided beading thread: FusionBeads.com. Clasp: Objects and Elements. 9mm Lucite rounds (sold as 10mm), 11mm Lucite rounds (sold as 12mm), and 13mm Lucite round (sold as 12mm): The Beadin' Path.

Constellations Necklace and Roped In Necklace
BY MELINDA BARTA (PAGE 96)

Maroon luster size 11° seed beads: The Bead Cache. Dark purple bronze luster size 11° seed beads: Bead Haven. All other seed beads: Beyond Beadery. Clasps, Swarovski bicones, and FireLine braided beading thread: FusionBeads.com. Pressed-glass rounds: Starman.

Rolling In the Deep and Design Option
BY JILL WISEMAN (PAGE 108)

Swarovski bicones, FireLine braided beading thread, and all other materials: Beyond Beadery.

Twisty-Turny and Design Option
BY JEAN POWER (PAGE 114)
DESIGN OPTION BY MELINDA BARTA

Swarovski crystals, Nymo nylon beading thread, and all other materials: Beads By Blanche. Green seed beads (in Design Option): Bead Haven. Cubes and drops: Beyond Beadery. Seed bead mix, memory wire, memory wire cutters, and peanut beads: FusionBeads.com. Lucite rounds: The Beadin' Path. Glass rondelle by Cynthia Craig: Goody Beads.

Buena Vista
BY LESLIE FRAZIER (PAGE 120)

Toho triangle beads, Delica cylinder beads, all other seed beads, FireLine braided beading thread, and Swarovski bicones, rounds, and pearl: Out On A Whim.

Anything Goes and Design Option
BY MELINDA BARTA (PAGE 136)

Miyuki drops, FireLine braided beading thread, and all other seed beads: Beyond Beadery. Peanut beads: Knot Just Beads. Keith O'Connor raku rounds: Green Girl Studios, The Beadin' Path, and eeBeads.com. Striped ceramic and polka dot ceramic beads: Golem Design Studio. End caps: Silk Road Treasures. Bronze clasp hook: Objects and Elements. Copper clasp hook: Ornamentea. Artistic craft wire (sold as gunmetal) and seed beads in red/purple colorway: FusionBeads.com.

Girasole and Design Options
BY LISA KAN (PAGE 142)

Seed beads and Swarovski marguerite flower (article #3700): Out On A Whim. Vintage bronze wire: Parawire. FireLine braided beading thread: Bass Pro Shops.

Paisley Paillettes and Semiprecious Paisley Necklace
BY MELINDA BARTA (PAGE 150)

Seed beads, FireLine braided beading thread, and One-G beading thread: Beyond Beadery. 4×3mm glass rondelles: Luna's Beads and Glass. 8×5mm glass rondelles: April Melody. Labradorite and garnet beads: Bead Trust. Similar 8×5mm glass rondelles, gauged wire, and Softflex beading wire: FusionBeads.com. Box clasp (used in necklace; not shown): Let It Bead.

START SHOPPING

Check your local bead shop or contact the companies below to purchase the materials used in this book. Your local bead shop may be able to order from the wholesale-only companies for you. See Project Resources on page 164 for a list of materials for each project.

A Grain of Sand
PO Box 3214
Mooresville, NC 28117
(704) 660-3125
agrainofsand.com

Applegate Lapidary
30 Main St.
Sutter Creek, CA 95685
(209) 267-9882
applegatelapidary.com

April Melody
beads@aprilmelody.com
aprilmelody.com

Arbeads.com
11901 137th Ave. Ct. KPN
Gig Harbor, WA 98329
(866) 715-2323
artbeads.com

Bass Pro Shops
(800) 227-7776
basspro.com

The Bead Cache
3307 S. College Ave.,
Unit 105
Fort Collins, CO 80525
(970) 224-4322
bead-cache.com

Bead Haven
925 S. Main St.
Frankenmuth, MI 48734
(989) 652-3566
beadhaven.com

Bead Parlor
423 Pine St.
Fort Morgan, CO 80701
(719) 320-2059
beadparlor.com

Bead Trust
649 Anderson St.
Charlotte, NC 28205
(704) 375-2545
beadtrust.com

Bead World
8 S. Brockway
Palatine, IL 60067
(877) 802-2401
beadworldbeads.com

The Beadin' Path
15 Main St.
Freeport, ME 04032
(877) 922-3237
beadinpath.com

The BeadSmith
(wholesale only)
37 Hayward Ave.
Carteret, NJ 07008
(732) 969-5300
beadsmith.com

Beads by Blanche
160 N. Washington Ave.
Bergenfield, NJ 07621
(201) 385-6225
beadsbyblanche.com

Beaux Beads
beauxbeads.etsy.com

Beyond Beadery
PO Box 460
Rollinsville, CO 80474
(800) 840-5548
beyondbeadery.com

Charlene's Beads
(760) 530-9436
cbbeads.com

eeBeads.com
(888) 746-7382
eebeads.com

FusionBeads.com
3830 Stone Wy. N.
Seattle, WA 98103
(888) 781-3559
fusionbeads.com

Green Girl Studios
PO Box 19389
Asheville, NC 28815
(828) 298-2263
greengirlstudios.com

Golem Design Studio
(623) 707-3267
golemstudio.com

Goody Beads
15105 Minnetonka
Industrial Rd.
Ste. 111
Minnetonka, MN 55345
(952) 938-2324
goodybeads.com

INM Crystal
2463 Quantum Blvd.
Boynton Beach, FL
33426
(561) 734-2101
inmcrystal.com

Jo-Ann Fabric and Craft Stores
(888) 739-4120
joann.com

Kabela Design
188 Kingswood Ct.
Glen Mills, PA 19342
(610) 459-5816
kabeladesign.com

Knot Just Beads
4309 S. 76th St.
Greenfield, WI 53220
(414) 771-8360
knotjustbeads.com

Leather Cord, USA
509 Hickory Ridge Trl.,
Ste. 110
Woodstock, GA 30188
(877) 700-2673
leathercordusa.com

Let It Bead
821 Englewood Pkwy.
Englewood, CO 80110
(303) 788-1466
letitbeadcolorado.com

Luna's Beads and Glass
416 Main St.
Frisco, CO 80424
(970) 668-8001
lunasbeads.com

Melinda Barta
melinda@melindabarta.com
melindabarta.com

Objects and Elements
16128 Old Snohomish-
Monroe Rd.
Snohomish, WA 98290
(206) 965-0373
objectsandelements.com

Ornamentea
509 N. West St.
Raleigh, NC 27603
(919) 834-6260
ornamentea.com

Out On A Whim
121 E. Cotati Ave.
Cotati, CA 94931
(800) 232-3111
whimbeads.com

Parawire
2–8 Central Ave.
East Orange, NJ 07018
(973) 672-0500
parawire.com

Primitive Earth Beads & Chain
5217 8th Ave. S.
Gulfport, FL. 33707
(800) 777-0038
pebeads.com

Rishashay
PO Box 8271
Missoula, MT 59807
(800) 517-3311
rishashay.com

Silk Road Treasures
28566 Ballard Dr.,
Unit C
Lake Forest, IL 60045
(866) 775-7710
silkroadtreasures.com

Starman
(wholesale only)
250 Center Park Wy.
Sequim, WA 98382
(888) 683-2323
czechbeads.com

Tapestry Beads
(512) 663-8385
tapestrybeads.com

Terri Caspary Schmidt
casparylampwork@yahoo.com
casparylampwork.com

Vintaj Natural Brass Co.
(wholesale only)
PO Box 246
Galena, IL 61036
(815) 776-0481
vintaj.com

The Whole Bead Shop
PO Box 1100
Nevada City, CA 95959
(800) 796-5350
wholebeadshop.com

INDEX

expand your
jewelry collection

with these essential resources from Interweave

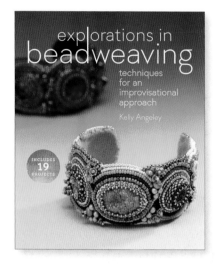

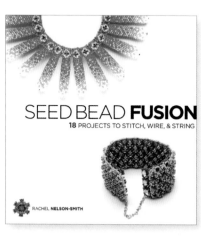